The Price Tag

Are Congregants Now Paying for the Word? Volume I

D'Morea Johnson

In Loving Memory of

My Mother

Denise D. Marks

March 10, 1952 – June 9, 2005

A former Congregant of:

The Friendly Baptist Church
(Bronx, New York)

Pilgrim Cathedral of Harlem
(New York, New York)

The Lord's Church Family Worship Center
(Bronx, New York)

Her favorite experience as a believer was:
Holy Communion
Final Scripture found on her Bible:
(St. John 11: 25 & 26)

Jesus said unto her, I am the resurrection, and the life: he that believeth in me, though he were dead, yet shall he live: And whosoever liveth and believeth in me shall never die. Believest thou this?

"It is your Father's good pleasure to give you the Kingdom" (Luke 12:32)

But today, many of our ministry leaders are trying to sell us the Kingdom!

Controversy for the discerning believer...

The Price Tag

Are Congregants Now Paying for the Word?

Volume I

D'Morea Johnson

Published by
Realmology Books, LLC.
*Atlanta   Toronto   London
Australia   Johannesburg

www.REALMOLOGYBOOKS.com

One Glenlake Parkway
Atlanta, Georgia 30328

A Subsidiary of The City of Realmology, LLC.

Copyright © 2005 by Realmology Books, LLC.

All rights reserved. Written permission must be secured from the publisher to use or reproduce any part of this book, except for brief quotations in critical reviews or articles.

Legal Claims/Litigation and/or requests for permission to reproduce material from this work should be sent to:

The City of Realmology, LLC.
c/o Legal Affairs
P.O. Box 77028
Atlanta, Georgia 30357

Unless otherwise noted, all Scripture quotations are from the King James Version and New King James Version.

Library of Congress Control Number: 2005902796
ISBN: 0-9765506-0-1 (Paperback-English)

Book Cover Design by Michael Cox
Edited by Shellie Hurrle and Sally D. Hyatt-Kearney
Layout/Design by D'Morea Johnson and Sally D. Hyatt-Kearney
Author's Photo by Jo Lance

This publication was written in New York City and Stamford, Connecticut

Printed in the United States of America

ACKNOWLEDGMENTS

I must begin by honoring God for doing such a tremendous work in and through my life! This publication has been a life-changing experience in a profound and most strategic way. I'm still amazed how a simple radio segment turned into a few lines of an email, and then became a few pages for a proposed magazine article, which then turned into this book. The Holy Spirit has proven throughout this entire journey to be Teacher. I give all Praise and Glory to His name, for He has done a great work for His people!

To all of my former pastors, I thank you for sowing the Word by impartation into my life that has been unquestionably nurtured, allowing me to pen this incredible publication through the Holy Spirit. I honor all of you for your stewardship, knowing the Spirit of Christ Jesus has equipped you to impart virtue into the lives of all of those He draws to your assemblies. The Most High God will continue to bless you, as you remain confident and determined for the Gospel's sake.

To Reverend Pat Reeves (Creative Enterprises) you have been a tremendous asset to this publication. Thank you for taking time out of your busy schedule to provide guidance and intercessory prayer. Thank you for an incredible Foreword and Prayer and all of the prior support throughout the years. God bless you with heaven's best as He continues to prosper you!
Visit http://www.thepatreevesstory.com

D'MOREA JOHNSON

To Michael Cox (Alpha Advertising), thank you for a great book design. Through the Spirit of God, you've been able to capture the message of this book most professionally. Thank you for your professionalism and talent. I'm glad we were able to do business together and I know others will be able to experience the same creative and artistic approach when consulting with your company to do business. I am sure we will be working together again, God Bless You! For more information, visit http://www.alphaadvertising.com

To Senior Editor Shellie Hurrle and Sally D. Hyatt-Kearney. Thank you for your professionalism, as you've been able to retain/capture the sincerity of my voice. I appreciate your editing and proofing skills you've supplied, including consulting initiated during this project. You've met my timeline, answered questions, addressed concerns, and even offered additional information that I might find helpful. Thank you again, for your skill sets applied toward this publication. God Bless You!

To all who provided public information regarding Martin Luther, in particular Reverend Robert E. Smith (Electronic Resources Librarian), Concordia Theological Seminary, Mr. Ed Walsh (CRTA Center for Reformed Theology and Apologetics), visit http://www.reformed.org, Michigan State University (The Reformation Guide), Boston College (Portrait of Martin Luther) and KDG Wittenberg http://www.luther.de

To all believers who shared your most personal experiences to make this publication as relevant as it should be, I thank you for believing in this message and contributing from the broken areas of your lives. I honor your courage and strength that will never be forgotten or overlooked. God Bless You All!

CONTENTS

FOREWORD and PRAYER   i
PREFACE   vi
INTRODUCTION   ix
DEDICATION   xi
REFLECTION   xv
THE 95 THESES   xxiv

Chapter One
A CONGREGANT'S VOICE
1.1 Greetings   1
1.2 New York   4
1.3 Los Angeles   10
1.4 Las Vegas   26
1.5 Atlanta   31
1.6 Back to New York (Familiar Place–Needing God's Grace)   43

Chapter Two
IT'S OFFERING TIME IN THE SANCTUARY! (Applause)
2.1 Concerning Our Tithes and Offerings   78
2.2 Money and Prophecy Lines   87
2.3 The Seed Offering (Sowing into the Word)   99
2.4 Sacrificial Offerings, Vows, and Tainted Giving   107

Chapter Three
THE CHURCH
3.1 Order of Worship Changes (Big Business/Less Ministry)   115
3.2 Materialism and Spirituality/Mentality (Who's Really Prospering?)   124
3.3 No Refuge   134
3.4 Mentors (Spiritual Fathers and Role Models)   142

Chapter Four
MASS MEDIA EVANGELISM
4.1 Paid Programming   **148**
     (Televangelism and Radio Ministry)
4.2 eMinistry and Virtual Pastors   **158**
4.3 The Fight for the Tithe   **166**
4.4 Partnering   **169**
     (Direct Mail Solicitation and Telemarketing)

Chapter Five
REACHING IN FOR OUTREACH—TAKING OUT FOR PROFIT
5.1 Community Choirs and Recording Groups   **179**
5.2 Stage Plays and Productions   **186**
5.3 Outreach and Missions   **193**
     (Domestic and International)

Chapter Six
AUTHOR'S DELIBERATION
6.1 Calling All Members of the Body of Christ   **202**
6.2 Get Your House in Order: "The Ministry Bureau"   **209**
     (Serving Those Who Serve)
6.3 Our Leaders   **215**

AUTHOR'S BIO   **225**
REPRESENTATION   **226**
AUTHOR'S CONTACT INFORMATION   **226**

FOREWORD and PRAYER

Reverend Pat Reeves

Readers, are you ready? I challenge you to embrace a profound and most needed message that will encourage your heart. History is indeed repeating itself! Using a comparison from a powerful message delivered in the sixteenth century, now to experience a reflective message in this, the twenty-first century, I'm absolutely positive, there are going to be changes impacting assemblies all around the world.

A great voice was heard and a cry was made for a radical revolution in 1517 in the person of Martin Luther (1483-1546), a German monk and ordained priest. The alarm was sounded when he penned *The 95 Theses*, which opposed the Wittenberg Church and its practices. Martin Luther's symbolic blow and gallant stance began the reformation, altering the course of Christianity forever, and he'll always be remembered as *The Great Revolutionary* and *Reformer of the Protestant Movement*.

His document contained an attack on papal abuse and the sale of indulgences by church officials. Luther saw the reformation as having a greater importance than a revolution against ecclesiastical abuse; he believed it was a fight for the Gospel. How many people are willing to fight for the Gospel? He would have been content yielding every point of dispute to the Pope, if only the Pope had affirmed the Gospel! The sincerity of the Gospel, in his estimation, was the doctrine of justification by faith, teaching that Christ's own righteousness is imputed to those who believe; having this position, God accepts them!

Well, God has in this twenty-first century summoned another voice in the person of journalist and author D'Morea Johnson to sound the alarm once again, to pen the truth, the whole truth, and nothing but the truth. He embraces this powerful message, becoming a reformer and revolutionary in his own right! Proclaiming a subtle yet complex and immensely influential statement, magnifying the voice of the late Martin Luther, raising the question, *Are Congregants Now Paying for the Word?*

This voice mirrors many concerns that penetrated hearts in the sixteenth century; and even today, the twenty-first century, as believers' lives are becoming broken and used, and they are being taken advantage of—growing distant from the things of God, including our ministry leaders. This international voice places a stamp in the hearts of all believers, as *The Price Tag* is proclaimed to stir up the souls of millions.

Congregants, including those that serve in ministry, will be impacted by this message, exposing this major dilemma affecting millions of believers. As millions will be liberated, changed, and freed from bondages placed by ministries at large, causing congregants to now THINK (using wisdom); no longer surrendering their mind power to others, telling them what to do with their own money! So as you approach this life-changing message, allow the Holy Spirit to govern your thinking, and obtain understanding, compassion and even forgiveness for those who have been or still are mistreating God's beloved people. It's time to WAKE UP, my brothers and sisters, now positioning ourselves to begin strengthening the Body of Christ! This message/voice truly becomes the modern-day Martin Luther, being a reformer and revolutionary to and for the Body of Christ!

Let us pray: Father who art in heaven, while beholding everything on earth, hallowed be your name. Worthy, Honorable, Laudable, Glorious, and Righteous are your name. You have called once again and someone has answered; he has said Yes to Your Will, Yes to Your Way, and Yes to the Work you've assigned to his hands. Loud cries, weary tears, and maltreated voices of your sons and daughters have presented themselves before you because they've been internally wounded, specifically targeted, emotionally abused, tempted, harassed, intimidated, and taken advantage of!

As a result, Father, your people are experiencing suffocation in the Body of Christ; many are losing their lives, losing their homes, having demolished relationships. They are financially robbed by our spiritual leaders–and are challenged by spiritual self-esteem resulting in lack of confidence in your Word, which is destroying believers' Faith!

Thank you, Father, for responding to our grievances; thank you, Father, for calling another one of your sons to be a divine bullhorn to utter the truth-releasing peace, happiness, and joy, including *The Joy of Giving,* bringing it back into the lives of we, your people!

- You arise, Oh God, through *The Price Tag* and let every hireling be scattered.

- You arise, Oh God, through *The Price Tag* and let every wolf in shepherd's clothing be revealed.

- You arise, Oh God, through *The Price Tag* and let every charlatan, imposter, trickster, and masquerader be disclosed.

- You arise, Oh God, through *The Price Tag,* destroying and eradicating forever the doctrine of No Money-No Blessing, No Money-No Healing, No Money-No Miracle.

- You arise, Oh God, through *The Price Tag* and let every gimmick, stunt, device, and scheme be obliterated.

- You arise, Oh God, through *The Price Tag,* opening the eyes of your sons and daughters so we will rightly discern truth from error and be cognizant of what is and what is not of You!

- You arise, Oh God, and let every son and daughter in the Body of Christ who has been financially, mentally, and emotionally duped, hoodwinked, manipulated, drained, and robbed be restored, healed, renewed, invigorated, empowered, strengthened, and reestablished.

- You arise, Oh God, and unveil to those you've called, anointed, appointed to preach, teach, prophecy, and evangelize (winning the lost souls of men and women), becoming penitent, seeking hard after you for pardon and forgiveness, for many have become intoxicated with greed. (The errors of their ways)

THE PRICE TAG

- You arise, Oh God, and bring an end (through the Truth of Your Word) to the practice of obtaining material possession, fame, and success at the destruction of others, while giving nothing in return but empty words, promissory notes, crafted and/or scripted speeches having no virtue!

- You arise, Oh God, and let Your wisdom, understanding, and truth permeate the Body of Christ in the name of Jesus, The Hero of the Church, Our Lord and Master, The Way, The Truth, and The Life. Amen!

PREFACE

How many powerful sermons have we heard about Jesus empowering believers to do great and exceeding things in and through him? Well, when are we going to realize He wasn't lying? The power that works within us isn't limited to only defeating situations that seem impossible, but it helps us to stand against all things that present themselves as an enemy! Although, our fellow brothers and sisters in Christ Jesus will never become our enemies, we have a major situation at hand regarding a force that has entered our realm, displaying enemy characteristics. The purpose of this book is to bring unquestioning awareness to believers, non-believers including all supporters of ministry! This international message doesn't stem from a spirit that seeks to unleash attack on the Church. This message is a bold and relevant subject; we must do our best not to allow it to cause interruption within the sacred walls of our sanctuaries and ministries.

Millions of congregants are attending church, watching Christian televised programming, having hidden frustration regarding several areas of ministry! With no voice for many decades, believers began praying regarding an overwhelming number of concerns. We serve a God that perfects the concerns of His people; therefore, we must realize He isn't going to sit back allowing His beloved/chosen people (the sheep of His pasture) to have continual heartache during a serious day as this.

Church is a relevant part of my life, providing privileges for praise and worship, biblical studies, and also at times, opportunities to exercise my gifts and talents. The course of my life has been an interesting journey traveling, and including relocating to different cities in America. From New York to Los Angeles, Las Vegas and Atlanta, returning to New York over a decade later (writing this book) then to return to Atlanta (where I reside), has offered intriguing experiences and many lessons learned! My exposure to several ministries has rewarded me, yet also scared me in some areas of my life.

In 1999, the Holy Spirit showed me some areas of my life that were affected negatively by ministry, which may sound strange. Of course, the services we render unto God isn't what affects the lives of individuals, but it's those that lead/govern us into the directions in which we serve. I seemed to have developed an approach for dealing with aspects of church and outreach ministries. Once we've learned and experienced the dealings behind the scenes, sometimes our mindset changes from the average congregant's experience; thereafter, the seed of this book was planted and then nurtured slowly!

Although a journalist, my approach to this book wasn't to become another voice in media waiting for an opportunity to expose a scandal surrounding preachers, religion, and the Church. This message clearly echoes as a voice of a congregant having a motive to reach fellow believers offering sound awareness. As your brother in Christ Jesus, it has taken several years to nurture the approach of this publication, and the journey of my life has helped me gain understanding of a great work that is purposed! How many more lives are we going to lose before congregants realize false hope must be exposed? How many more believers are going to turn their backs on the Church, including God, because our assemblies are becoming corrupt? How long are we going to sit back while many of our leaders are premeditating how to manipulate us, knowing accountability within ministry doesn't exist? How many more believers are going be abused, deceived and turned away after being victimized from leaders not in position to serve God, but serving themselves?

INTRODUCTION

Remember the last time you were shopping for a new outfit in a department store? Wasn't it challenging finding the right color, size, etc.? But do you also remember the day you ran across a new ensemble that just took you by surprise, leaving you puzzled as you wondered what shoes and accessories would match? This kind of experience instantaneously grabs your attention, especially when you find the right color and size. You pull it off the rack, turn it around, observe the fabric, and admire the style and materials. I'm sure this type of department store experience doesn't happen often.

Would that experience resemble church today? Are you excited about receiving the Word—its delivery, style, and principals? Just as in the department store, after you've become so excited about what you've found, there is always one thing dangling from the sleeve, and that's the price tag! Millions of congregants now believe their assemblies aren't much different. After becoming excited about what they've received, there is now one thing dangling from the mouth of the man or woman of God and that is a seed offering. **Are congregants now paying for the Word of God? Are men and women of God now marketing FREE principals from The Bible?**

Remember when believers' uplifted hands and/or by touching and agreeing, symbolized the act of receiving from God? Well today, congregants are solicited to SOW into the preached Word, symbolizing the planting of finances in faith and hope of reaping a harvest! To those who believe, **Seed Time and Harvest** is an embraced Kingdom principal for living, but controversy has arisen as congregants feel as if they're now tipping, giving a gratuity, to declare, "I believe and/or receive."

This book is a must have for every preacher/teacher, tither, congregant, choir member, praise and worship leader, trustee, usher, and all supporters of ministry. It truly outlines, as well as enlightens, the understanding of millions regarding **Sanctuary Worship Services, Mega-Churches, Televangelism, Outreach and Missions**, and more. A silent cry now escapes the hearts of millions of congregants, even those that serve in ministry, who are feeling prostituted while funding the House and leadership! Congregants are turning away from their assemblies and even God, settling for a Christian lifestyle without a pastor, because a reflection of the latter days of indulgences has ambushed the Church yet again, or rather have become re-modernized!

DEDICATION

What is a backslider, or rather what categorizes an individual as a backslider? The word backslider is found in the book of (Proverbs 14:14), but I'm searching for a profound definition to better understand its meaning. Would the definition appear as a category the Church has created to classify the present status of a believer? Are there several determining factors when classifying someone as a backslider? Or would the determination become situational according to reason, purpose, or decision to become a backslider?

Would a backslider be a person who believes on the name of the Lord and then later changes his or her mind no-longer believing? Would a backslider be a believer who strays away from his or her church because of rules and regulations, including legalism of religion, which contradicts the lifestyle of an individual? Would a backslider be an individual who has slowly progressed away from some aspects of the Christian lifestyle? Or would a backslider be a believer who purposely chooses to stay home and worship God because sanctuary environments are growing more and more corrupt?

I'm becoming a little confused as to what determines classification of a backslider! From my experience, I know for certain that many of us have been in one of these categories at some time or another, but for some reason, there are an increasing number of individuals backsliding purposely! Yes, believers are choosing to backslide on purpose, having a motive to protect themselves from an intimidating force that has ambushed our assemblies!

May I continue by saying I'm sorry? I feel the urgency to open this dedication with an apology! I must apologize on behalf of pastors and ministry leaders who have allowed congregants to stray. I pray you're able to receive in your hearts this apology on behalf of those who were and still are not able to stand before us (yes, I said *us*) and say, "I'm sorry!" This book is dedicated to millions of current and former congregants who retain frustration regarding the Church. There are so many believers around the world wandering without a pastor! Not because they're stubborn and don't want to support ministry, but because many churches are now operating outside its sacred establishment!

Church has always been the place for healing, reconciliation and impartation, but there is no ministry for those that live in pain inflicted upon the Church. Where are the sheep to go, whom are we to call? Year after year, thousands of believers begin wandering either from church to church, or astray, seeking emotional or spiritual healing. Some still retain love for God, maintaining scheduled time for studying and praise and worship, now behind the comforting doors of their homes. As many have fallen far away from their embraced religion, there are those that still sit silently, hurting, crying, and seeking God for real answers!

I'm dedicating this book to those who have no voice, but desire to stand against what they know in their hearts is wrong! It's my prayer that former and current congregants will begin waking up, striving to get the House of prayer back in order! God has heard your cry, my brother, and my sister. He is ready to bring order back into His House, but you must remember *YOU ARE*

THE PRICE TAG

THE CHURCH, THE BODY OF CHRIST; therefore YOU must allow what's within YOU (the Holy Spirit) to proclaim a voice that is so needed today, thereby bringing order back where it belongs! ***"Let the words of my mouth and the meditation of my heart be acceptable in your sight, oh Lord, my strength and my redeemer."*** Amen!

REFLECTION

Martin Luther 1483-1546

Martin Luther, German theologian and religious reformer, initiated the Protestant Reformation, and his vast influence, extending beyond religion to politics, economics, education, and language, has made him one of the crucial figures in modern European history. Luther was born in Eisleben on November 10, 1483. He was descended from the peasantry, a fact he often stressed. His father, Hans Luther, was a copper miner in the mining area of Mansfeld. Luther received a sound primary and secondary education at Mansfeld, Magdeburg, and Eisenach. In 1501, at the age of 17, he enrolled at the University of Erfurt, receiving a bachelor's degree in 1502 and a master's degree in 1505.

He then intended to study law, as his father wished, In July of that year, however, he narrowly escaped death in a thunderstorm and vowed to become a monk. The decision surprised his friends and appalled his father. He entered the monastery of the Augustinian Hermits at Erfurt. Although he observed the rules imposed on a novice, he did not find the peace of God he was expecting. Nevertheless, Luther made his profession as a monk in the fall of 1506, and his superiors selected him for the priesthood; he was ordained in 1507.

After his ordination, Luther was asked to study theology in order to become a professor at one of the many new German universities staffed by monks. In 1508, he was assigned by Johann von Staupitz, vicar-general of the Augustinians and a friend and counselor, to the new University of Wittenberg (founded in 1502) to give introductory lectures in moral philosophy. He received his bachelor's degree in theology in 1509 and returned to Erfurt, where he taught and studied (1509-1511). In November 1510, on behalf of seven Augustinian monasteries, he made a visit to Rome, where he performed the religious duties customary for a pious visitor and was shocked by the worldliness of the Roman clergy. Soon after resuming his duties in Erfurt, he was reassigned to Wittenberg and asked to study for the degree of doctor of theology.

In 1512, he received his doctorate and took over the chair of biblical theology, which he held until his death. Luther was well acquainted with the scholastic theology of his day, but he made the study of the Bible, especially the epistles of Saint Paul, the center of his work.

THE PRICE TAG

Luther found that his teachings diverged increasingly from the traditional beliefs of the Roman Church. His studies had led him to the conclusion that Christ was the sole mediator between God and man and that forgiveness of sin and salvation are affected by God's grace alone (*sola gratia*) and are received by faith alone (*sola fide*) on the part of man. This point of view turned him against scholastic theology, which had emphasized man's role in his own salvation, and the necessity of the Church for salvation.

Here consisted the essential break between Luther and the medieval church. He did not deny the role of the Church as an instrument of God; what he denied was the widely held belief that salvation was impossible outside of it. He saw the emphasis on penitential exercises and other good works as unhealthy and even useless for one who could see himself as a sinner justified by God himself.

The doctrine of indulgences, with its mechanical view of sin and repentance, aroused Luther's indignation. The sale by the Church of indulgences—the remission of temporal punishments for sins committed and confessed to a priest—brought in much revenue. The archbishop of Mainz, Albert of Brandenburg, sponsored such a sale in 1517 to pay the pope for his appointment to Mainz and for the construction of Saint Peter's in Rome. He selected Johann Tetzel, a Dominican friar, to preach the indulgences and collect the revenues. When Tetzel arrived in Saxony, Luther posted his famous *95 Theses* on the door of the castle church at Wittenberg on October 31, 1517. Although some of the theses directly criticized papal policies, they were put forward as tentative objections for discussion.

Copies of *The 95 Theses* were quickly spread throughout Europe, unleashing a storm of controversy. During 1518 and 1519, Luther defended his theology before his fellow Augustinians and publicly debated in Leipzig with the theologian Johann Eck, who had condemned the ideas of Luther. Meanwhile, church officials acted against him. The Saxon Dominican provincial charged him with heresy, and he was summoned to appear in Augsburg before the papal legate, Cardinal Cajetan. Refusing to recant, he fled to Wittenberg, seeking the protection of the elector Frederick III of Saxony.

When the Wittenberg faculty sent a letter to Frederick declaring its solidarity with Luther, the elector refused to send Luther to Rome, where he would certainly meet imprisonment or death.

In 1520, Luther completed three celebrated works in which he stated his views. In his *Address to the Christian Nobility of the German Nation*, he invited the German princes to take the reform of the Church into their own hands; in *A Prelude Concerning the Babylonian Captivity of the Church*, he attacked the papacy and the current theology of sacraments; and in *On the Freedom of a Christian*, he stated his position on justification and good works. The bull of pope Leo X, *Exsurge Domine*, issued on June 15 that same year, gave Luther sixty days to recant, and *Decet Romanum Pontificem* on January 3, 1521, excommunicated him.

Summoned to appear before Emperor Charles V at the Diet of Worms in April 1521, he was asked before the assembled secular and ecclesiastical rulers to recant. He refused firmly, asserting that he would have to be convinced by Scripture and clear reason in order to do so, and that going against conscience is not safe for anyone. (The statement "Here I stand; I cannot do otherwise," traditionally attributed to him, is most likely legendary.)

THE PRICE TAG

Condemned by the emperor, Luther was spirited away by his prince, the elector Frederick the Wise of Saxony, and kept in hiding at Wartburg Castle. There he began his translation of the New Testament from the original Greek into German, a seminal contribution to the development of a standard German language. Disorders in Wittenberg caused by some of his more extreme followers forced his return to the city in March 1521, and he restored peace through a series of sermons.

Luther continued his teaching and writing in Wittenberg but soon became involved in the controversies surrounding the Peasants' War (1524-1526) because the leaders of the peasants originally justified their demands with arguments somewhat illegitimately drawn from his writings. He considered their theological arguments false, although he supported many of their political demands. When the peasants turned violent, he angrily denounced them and supported the princes' effort to restore order. Although he later repudiated the harsh, vengeful policy adopted by the nobles, his attitude toward the war lost him many friends.

In the midst of this controversy, in 1525, he married Katharina von Bora, a former nun. The marriage was happy, and his wife became an important supporter in his busy life. After having articulated his basic theology in his earlier writings, he published the *Small Catechism*, his most popular book, in 1529. By commenting briefly in question and answer form on the Ten Commandments, the Apostles' Creed, the Lord's Prayer, Baptism, and the Lord's Supper, the *Small Catechism* explains the theology of the evangelical reformation in simple yet colorful language. Not allowed to attend the Diet of Augsburg because he had been banned and excommunicated, Luther had to leave the presentation of the reformers' position (formulated in the Augsburg Confession, 1530) to his friend and colleague Philipp Melanchthon. In 1532,

Luther's translation of the Old Testament from the original Hebrew was published. Meanwhile, his influence spread across northern and eastern Europe. His advocacy of the independence of rulers from ecclesiastical supervision won him the support of many princes (and was later interpreted in ways contrary to his original intention). His fame made Wittenberg an intellectual center.

By 1537, Luther's health had begun to deteriorate, and he felt burdened by the resurgence of the papacy and conflict with a radical wing of the reformers, the Anabaptists. In the winter of 1546, Luther was asked to settle a controversy between two young counts that ruled the area of Mansfeld, where he had been born.

Old and sick, he went there, resolved the conflict, and died on February 18, 1546, in Eisleben. Luther was not a systematic theologian, but his work was subtle, complex, and immensely influential. It was inspired by his careful study of the New Testament, but it was also influenced in important respects by the great fourth-century theologian St. Augustine. Luther's theological ideas can be summarized as follows:

Law and Gospel

Luther maintained that God interacts with human beings in two ways—through the law and through the Gospel! The law represents God's demands as expressed, for example, in the Ten Commandments and of the golden rule. All people, regardless of their religious convictions, have some degree of access to the law through their consciences and through the ethical traditions of their culture, although their understanding of it is always distorted by human sin. The law has two functions. It enables human beings to maintain some order in their world, their communities, and their own lives, despite the profound alienation from God, the world, their neighbors, and ultimately what is caused by original sin. In addition, the law makes human beings aware of their need for the forgiveness of sins and thus leads them to Christ.

God also interacts with human beings through the Gospel, the good news of God's gift of his Son for the salvation of the human race. This proclamation demands nothing but acceptance on the part of the individual. Indeed, Luther argued that theology had gone wrong precisely when it began to confuse law and Gospel (God's demand and God's gift) by claiming that human beings can in some way merit that which can only be the unconditional gift of God's grace.

Sin

Luther insisted that Christians, as long as they live in this world, are sinners and saints simultaneously. They are saints insofar as they trust in God's grace and not in their own achievements. Sin, however, is a permanent and pervasive feature in the Church as well as in the world, and a saint is not a moral paragon but a sinner who accepts God's grace. Thus, for Luther, the most respected citizen and the habitual criminal are both in need of forgiveness by God.

The Finite and Infinite

Luther held that God makes himself known to human beings through earthly, finite forms rather than in his pure divinity. Thus, God revealed himself in Jesus Christ, He speaks His Word to us in the human words of the New Testament writers, and His Body and Blood are received by believers (in Luther's formulation, called consubstantiation) and under the bread and wine in Holy Communion. When human beings serve each other and the world in their various occupations (which Luther called vocations) as mothers and fathers, rulers and subjects, butchers and bakers, they are instruments of God, who works in the world through them. Luther thus broke down the traditional distinction between sacred and secular occupations.

THE PRICE TAG

Theology of the Cross

Luther asserted that Christian theology is the theology of the cross rather than a theology of glory. Human beings cannot apprehend God by means of philosophy or ethics; they must let God be God and see him only where he chooses to make himself known. Thus, Luther stressed that God reveals his wisdom through the foolishness of preaching, his power through suffering, and the secret of meaningful life through Christ's death on the cross.

THE 95 THESES

A perfect reflection of one that has come before us. Let us revisit the message of Martin Luther.

Martin Luther

(Translated from Latin to English)

DISPUTATION OF DOCTOR MARTIN LUTHER ON THE POWER AND EFFICACY OF INDULGENCES OCTOBER 31, 1517

1. When our Lord and Master Jesus Christ said, "Repent" (Matthew 4:17), he willed the entire life of believers to be one of repentance.
2. This word cannot be understood as referring to the sacrament of penance, that is, confession and satisfaction, as administered by the clergy.
3. Yet it does not mean solely inner repentance; such inner repentance is worthless unless it produces various outward mortification of the flesh.
4. The penalty of sin remains as long as the hatred of self (that is, true inner repentance), namely till our entrance into the Kingdom of Heaven.
5. The pope neither desires nor is able to remit any penalties except those imposed by his own authority or that of the canons.
6. The pope cannot remit any guilt, except declaring and showing that have remitted it by God, or, to be sure, by remitting guilt in cases reserved to his judgment. If his right to grant remission in these cases were disregarded, the guilt would certainly remain unforgiving.
7. God remits guilt to no one unless at the same time he humbles him in all things and makes him submissive to the vicar, the priest.

THE PRICE TAG

8. The penitential canons are imposed only on the living, and according to the canons themselves; nothing should be imposed on the dying.
9. Therefore, the Holy Spirit through the pope is kind to us insofar as the pope in his decrees always makes exception of the article of death and of necessity.
10. Those priests act ignorantly and wickedly and in the case of the dying, reserve canonical penalties for purgatory.
11. Those tares of changing the canonical penalty to the penalty of purgatory were evidently sown while the bishops slept (Matthew 13:25).
12. In former times, canonical penalties were imposed, not after but before absolution, as tests of true contrition.
13. The dying are freed by death from all penalties, are already dead as far as the canon laws are concerned, and have a right to be released from them.
14. Imperfect piety or love on the part of the dying person necessarily brings with it great fear, and the smaller the love, the greater the fear.
15. This fear or horror is sufficient in itself, to say nothing of other things, to constitute the penalty of purgatory, since it is very near to the horror of despair.
16. Hell, purgatory, and heaven seem to differ the same as despair, fear, and assurance of salvation.
17. It seems as though for the souls in purgatory, fear should necessarily decrease and love increase.
18. Furthermore, it does not seem proved, either by reason or by Scripture that souls in purgatory are outside the state of merit, that is, unable to grow in love.
19. Nor does it seem proved that souls in purgatory, at least not all of them, are certain and assured of their own salvation, even if we ourselves may be entirely certain of it.

20. Therefore, the pope, when he uses the words "plenary remission of all penalties," does not actually mean "all penalties," but only those imposed by him.
21. Thus, those indulgence preachers are in error when they say that a man is absolved from every penalty and saved by papal indulgences.
22. As a matter of fact, the pope remits to souls in purgatory no penalty, which, according to canon law, they should have paid in this life.
23. If remission of all penalties whatsoever could be granted to anyone at all, certainly it would be granted only to the most perfect, that is, to very few.
24. For this reason, most people are necessarily deceived by that indiscriminate and high-sounding promise of release from penalty.
25. That power, which the pope has in general over purgatory, corresponds to the power which any bishop or curate has in a particular way in his own diocese and parish.
26. The pope does very well when he grants remission to souls in purgatory, not by the power of the keys, which he does not have, but by way of intercession for them.
27. They preach only human doctrines that say that as soon as the money clinks into the money chest, the soul flies out of purgatory.
28. It is certain that when money clinks in the money chest, greed/avarice can be increased, but when the Church intercedes, the result is in the hands of God alone.
29. Who knows whether all souls in purgatory wish to be redeemed, since we have exceptions in St. Severinus and St. Paschal, as related in a legend?
30. No one is sure of the integrity of his own contrition, much less of having received plenary remission.
31. The man who actually buys indulgences is as rare as he who is really penitent; indeed, he is exceedingly rare.

THE PRICE TAG

32. Those who believe that they can be certain of their salvation because they have indulgence letters will be eternally damned, together with their teachers.
33. Men must especially be on guard against those who say that the pope's pardons are that inestimable gift of God by which man is reconciled to him.
34. For the graces of indulgences are concerned only with the penalties of sacramental satisfaction established by man.
35. They who teach that contrition is not necessary on the part of those who intend to buy souls out of purgatory or to buy confessional privileges preach unchristian doctrine.
36. Any truly repentant Christian has a right to full remission of penalty and guilt, even without indulgence letters.
37. Any true Christian, whether living or dead, participates in all the blessings of Christ and the Church, and God grants him this, even without indulgence letters.
38. Nevertheless, papal remission and blessing are by no means to be disregarded, for they are, as I have said (Thesis 6), the proclamation of the divine remission.
39. It is very difficult, even for the most learned theologians, at one and the same time to commend to the people the bounty of indulgences and the need of true contrition.
40. A Christian who is truly contrite seeks and loves to pay penalties for his sins; the bounty of indulgences, however, relaxes penalties and causes men to hate them—at least it furnishes occasion for hating them.
41. Papal indulgences must be preached with caution, lest people erroneously think that they are preferable to other good works of love.
42. Christians are to be taught that the pope does not intend that the buying of indulgences should in any way be compared with works of mercy.

43. Christians are to be taught that he who gives to the poor or lends to the needy does a better deed than he who buys indulgences.
44. Because love grows by works of love, man thereby becomes better. Man does not, however, become better by means of indulgences but is merely freed from penalties.
45. Christians are to be taught that he who sees a needy man and passes him by, yet gives his money for indulgences, does not buy papal indulgences but God's wrath.
46. Christians are to be taught that unless they have more than they need, they must reserve enough for their family needs and by no means squander it on indulgences.
47. Christians are to be taught that their buying of indulgences is a matter of free choice, not commanded.
48. Christians are to be taught that the pope, in granting indulgences, needs and thus desires their devout prayer more than their money.
49. Christians are to be taught that papal indulgences are useful only if they do not put their trust in them, but very harmful if they lose their fear of God because of them.
50. Christians are to be taught that if the pope knew the exactions of the indulgence preachers, he would rather that the Basilica of St. Peter were burned to ashes than built up with the skin, flesh, and bones of his sheep.
51. Christians are to be taught that the pope would and should wish to give of his own money, even though he had to sell the Basilica of St. Peter, to many of those from whom certain hawkers of indulgences cajole money.
52. It is vain to trust in salvation by indulgence letters, even though the indulgence commissary, or even the pope, was to offer his soul as security.

53. They are the enemies of Christ and the pope, who forbid altogether the preaching of the Word of God in some churches in order that indulgences may be preached in others.
54. Injury is done to the Word of God when, in the same sermon, an equal or larger amount of time is devoted to indulgences than to the Word.
55. It is certainly the pope's sentiment that if indulgences, which are a very insignificant thing, are celebrated with one bell, one procession, and one ceremony, then the gospel, which is the very greatest thing, should be preached with a hundred bells, a hundred processions, and a hundred ceremonies.
56. The true treasures of the Church, out of which the pope distributes indulgences, are not sufficiently discussed or known among the people of Christ.
57. That indulgences are not temporal treasures is certainly clear, for many indulgence sellers do not distribute them freely but only gather them.
58. Nor are they the merits of Christ and the saints, for, even without the pope, the latter always work grace for the inner man, and the cross, death and hell for the outer man.
59. St. Lawrence said that the poor of the Church were the treasures of the Church, but he spoke according to the usage of the word in his own time.
60. Without want of consideration, we say that the keys of the Church, given by the merits of Christ, are that treasure.
61. For it is clear that the pope's power is of itself sufficient for the remission of penalties and cases reserved by him.
62. The true treasure of the Church is the most Holy Gospel of the glory and grace of God.
63. But this treasure is naturally most odious, for it makes the first to be last (Matthew 20:16).

64. On the other hand, the treasure of indulgences is naturally most acceptable, for it makes the last to be first.
65. Therefore, the treasures of the gospel are nets with which one formerly fished for men of wealth.
66. The treasures of indulgences are nets with which one now fishes for the wealth of men.
67. The indulgences, which the demagogues acclaim as the greatest graces, are actually understood to be such only insofar as they promote gain.
68. They are nevertheless in truth the most insignificant graces when compared with the grace of God and the piety of the cross.
69. Bishops and curates are bound to admit the commissaries of papal indulgences with all reverence.
70. But they are much more bound to strain their eyes and ears lest these men preach there own dreams instead of what the pope has commissioned.
71. Let him who speaks against the truth concerning papal indulgences be anathema and accursed.
72. But let him who guards against the lust and license of the indulgence preachers be blessed.
73. Just as the pope justly thunders against those who by any mean whatsoever contrive harm to the sale of indulgences.
74. Much more does he intend to thunder against those who use indulgences as a pretext to contrive harm to holy love and truth.
75. To consider papal indulgences so great that they could absolve a man even if he had done the impossible and had violated the mother of God is madness.
76. We say on the contrary that papal indulgences cannot remove the very least of venial sins as far as guilt is concerned.
77. To say that even St. Peter, if he were now pope, could not grant greater graces is blasphemy against St. Peter and the pope.

78. We say on the contrary that even the present pope, or any pope whatsoever, has greater graces at his disposal, that is, the gospel, spiritual powers, gifts of healing, etc., as it is written (I Corinthians 12:28).
79. To say that the cross-emblazoned with the papal coat of arms and set up by the indulgence preachers is equal in worth to the cross of Christ is blasphemy.
80. The bishops, curates, and theologians who permit such talk to be spread among the people will have to answer for this.
81. This unbridled preaching of indulgences makes it difficult even for learned men to rescue the reverence, which is due the pope from slander or from the shrewd questions of the laity.
82. Such as: *Why does not the pope empty purgatory for the sake of holy love and the dire need of the souls that are there if he redeems an infinite number of souls for the sake of miserable money with which to build a church? The former reason would be most just; the latter is most trivial.*
83. Again, *Why are funeral and anniversary masses for the dead continued and why does he not return or permit the withdrawal of the endowments founded for them, since it is wrong to pray for the redeemed?*
84. Again, *What is this new piety of God and the pope that for a consideration of money they permit a man who is impious and their enemy to buy out of purgatory the pious soul of a friend of God and do not rather, because of the need of that pious and beloved soul, free it for pure love's sake?*
85. Again, *Why are the penitential canons, long since abrogated and dead in actual fact and through disuse, now satisfied by the granting of indulgences as though they were still alive and in force?*
86. Again, *Why does not the pope, whose wealth is today greater than the wealth of the richest Crassus, build this one Basilica of St. Peter with his own money rather than with the money of poor believers?*

87. Again, *What does the pope remit or grant to those who by perfect contrition already have a right to full remission and blessings?*
88. Again, *What greater blessing could come to the Church than if the pope were to bestow these remissions and blessings on every believer a hundred times a day, as he now does but once?*
89. Since the pope seeks the salvation of souls rather than money by his indulgences, why does he suspend the indulgences and pardons previously granted when they have equal efficacy?
90. To repress these very sharp arguments of the laity by force alone, and not to resolve them by giving reasons, is to expose the Church and the pope to the ridicule of their enemies and to make Christians unhappy.
91. If, therefore, indulgences were preached according to the Spirit and intention of the pope, all these doubts would be readily resolved. Indeed, they would not exist.
92. Away, then, with all those prophets who say to the people of Christ, "Peace, peace," and there is no peace! (Jeremiah 6:14).
93. Blessed be all those prophets who say to the people of Christ, "Cross, cross," and there is no cross!
94. Christians should be exhorted to be diligent in following Christ, and their Heads, through penalties, death and hell.
95. And thus be confident of entering into heaven through many tribulations rather than through the false security of peace (Acts 14:22)

CHAPTER ONE

A CONGREGANT'S VOICE

1.1 GREETINGS

WARNING:
This chapter details many actual events, allowing readers to understand the relevancy of the author's words; names and titles, including ministries and business entities, are listed to reflect relevancy. This information is not intended to cause harm or diminish any particular ministry, business or individual, but is listed as factual documentation for publication relevancy. Please view all information as educational and informative, usable within a group, classroom setting, church or other assembly!

Grace and peace be unto you from God our Father and the Lord Jesus Christ, I greet all my brothers and sisters from the Most High God who gives us His grace, mercy and peace. I believe this to be a great privilege, having the opportunity to communicate with you through this literary forum, discussing many crucial situations affecting the Christian community!

I should begin by telling you that I am not a theologian or a pastor, nor am I ordained with a recognizable title within the

Christian community. I'm just a congregant like many of you reading this book; over the past twenty-five years of my life I have been part of a few ministries in which I've been exposed to several doctrines and practices, from Baptist to Church of God in Christ (COGIC), from non-denominational to Pentecostal.

My experiences and exposure have set a course in my life that will be addressed in this book. From sanctuary worship services to outreach ministries, a community choir to having my own singing group, gospel stage plays to promoting events and more, I've become knowledgeable about the establishment and operations of what we call ministry in today's society. As a congregant, many times I suppressed anger, fear and frustration, not knowing to whom or where to turn. Most times during these experiences, it caused me to pull away from what I believed should have been maintained, in order to protect my feelings. I know millions have done the same thing; therefore, I'm earnest to communicate with you, making sure those who will come after us can choose a better way to handle the many crucial situations now affecting the Christian community!

Before we begin I think it's relevant to give honor where honor is due, as there is a profession that we often seem to forget. It's one of the most important and most needed occupations today. Have you forgotten your pastor, priest, bishop, elder, minister, evangelist or missionary? These men and women commit themselves to the services of millions through sanctuary worship services, outreach/missions and even broadcasted ministries. They teach our children as well as us, giving advice with spiritual guidance and biblical structures for a moral way of living! They counsel our families in times of need, baptize, join our loved ones in holy matrimony, and even speak encouraging and comforting words in times of bereavement. These powerful and most reverent individuals are instrumental in our lives, which we often forget to acknowledge.

Have you stopped to think about who takes the time to comfort and encourage our clergy in their time of need? Who do they call when in distress? Yes, we know clergy probably spend more time in prayer than most, but they are human as well. I'm sure they become weak, discouraged, lonely, sentimental, greedy, aroused, selfish, and angry just as we all do; sharing the same emotions we face daily. They're confronted with making right decisions and have to refrain from the wrong ones in order to avoid the consequences and effects of making the incorrect ones. *We all know clergy aren't perfect people*! Many have criminal histories, daily temptations, addictions, and more. So tell me, how do they handle their lives as human beings, while simultaneously continuing the service they offer to others?

It must be challenging to humble oneself to face individuals with similar problems and recognize their needs. It's mind-blowing to evaluate the circumstances they face in their own homes, communities, and the workplace and guess what, right in their own congregations. I'm certain there are those in their congregations who are having problems too. Congregations are made up of the same types of individuals from the surrounding communities we live in and faced with similar circumstances relating to sex, money, love, infidelity and other challenges.

Okay, let's be honest. Have you truly honored your clergyman or clergywoman's time rendered to your family week after week? It's a strenuous task to be of service to hundreds, possibly thousands, within a congregation, to maintain a functioning ministry solely dependent upon tax-deductible gifts and donations. It can most definitely become a bit troublesome when congregational members aren't supporting the ministry they use week after week.

But I guarantee congregants still expect the ministry to render service when needed!

It's my belief that congregants have taken advantage of our clergy for too long. We've become spoiled, expecting many things in our lives, expecting to be treated with dignity and respect. But what about those men and women who dedicated their lives in service to us? It begins to make our challenges look small, if at all even worthy! I am convinced that *clergy have the most important careers in the world*!

1.2 NEW YORK

I was born and raised in The Bronx, New York, and feel I was privileged to have been introduced to church, by my mother, at a young age. My church home was The Friendly Baptist Church (now called The Friendly Church), where my pastor was the Reverend Albert L. Sutton. Because I lived three blocks from the church, I remember seeing my pastor driving down the street and waving at members of the community. In my eyes, he was a great shepherd who cared for the sheep. He wasn't an angry man who used the Gospel to beat people down with rules and regulations, but was instead personable with his congregation, and judging from a recent visit in October 2004, nothing has changed.

It was a tremendous experience being away from the ministry for over ten years and then returning home to see my former pastor still walking the aisles, shaking hands, singing and fellowshipping with his congregation! He shook my hand before the service began and then acknowledged me to the congregation during morning worship service.

THE PRICE TAG

Offering was never a major deal in this community church. There were two separate offerings received: "Poor Saints Offering" and "Tithes and Offering." The only additional offering was when there was a visiting preacher, in which case a separate basket would appear. Reverend Sutton has been a blessing and has shown nothing less than what I believe a pastor should. He allowed me to exercise my gifts and talents and complimented me at times when others criticized. Naturally, there were occasions when Pastor Sutton and I didn't see eye to eye, such as when I was a teen and didn't make all the right decisions, and even as I evaluate myself today, I know I still don't!

Still, I learned at a very young age that pastors could get in the way of what God is formulating in the life of a believer. Around the age of sixteen, during a particular young adult choir rehearsal, I taught the choir an original song and even played it myself on the organ. The choir was extremely excited about this, as the ministry didn't have anyone teaching original music! After rehearsing it for nearly two weeks, we decided to sing it during Youth Day, which is typically the fifth Sunday on a quarterly calendar.

That Sunday morning Pastor Sutton asked to see me in his office, and I was puzzled as to why. Behind closed doors, he explained to me that there were paid musicians in the church, and I should not be playing the organ. He continued to state that he was going to allow me to play the organ that Sunday, but from then on, I was not to play it again! This instantly discouraged me from playing that morning, as my enthusiasm and that of the choir had disappeared.

I remember going home upset. I'd thought he would be excited that members possessed gifts and desired to share them with the ministry. But nevertheless, he was the authority of the House. On later occasions, there were other things I found discouraging as well. As of today, over fifteen years later, I have never played the organ inside another church, and I personally struggle so hard with myself when writing music for others. I found myself purchasing keyboards over the years but not being able to utilize them in the capacity I desired. I still have a strong desire to play but will have to focus myself differently regarding the desire that had been birthed previously.

When individuals find themselves trying to overcome particular fears, coaching is often required, for if we could overcome these fears ourselves, we would have done so by now! I believe Pastor Sutton had his personal reason(s), but because of his actions, there is now a handicapped believer who had at one time come forth to implement a gift to the Body of Christ only to be rejected! This behavior definitely came in the way of what God was and is formulating for my life. Many pastors don't realize their ability to build up...and definitely tear down. But as they always do, things change as year's progress; individuals have to grow and move on.

While a member of The Friendly Baptist Church, I joined an outreach-recording choir called Worship & Praise Mass Choir, under the direction of Minister Maharold Peoples Jr. I was probably about sixteen years old when I first joined, singing and frequently traveling from church to church (program to program) and occasionally out of town. This experience was exciting because it exposed me not only to the different varieties of gospel music, but also to other types of ministries—the denominational structures for what is titled church worship. I can recall several occasions when visiting different ministries where offering was a major deal, but later in this book, we will discuss each area in more specific detail.

Singing with an outreach choir requires dedication. You give so much of your personal time and a lot of your own money, and there is seldom any compensation. My pastor tried to warn me back in those days. While in his office, he shared a simple maxim:

THE PRICE TAG

How can you wash someone else's dishes when you have dirty dishes at home?

Although I brushed it off because I didn't understand what was entailed, I later realized that my commitment with the outreach choir probably did hinder my contributions to my home church. That was my first experience in realizing pastors' concerns when their members choose to support other ministries, thereby reducing their support of the House.

Minister Peoples worked very hard sharing his music ministry. Still, as I wasn't a lead singer in the choir, just a faithful member operating in the capacity afforded, I left the choir about two years later, feeling unappreciated. I never really complained about it, but I always felt it in my heart. I remember Minister Peoples joining a new church in Harlem and wanting the choir to participate in a crusade during the summer season. The choir was not there in full support because the crusade was a weeklong! I had arranged to leave work early. Because I maintained a part-time job in the evenings, I knew I couldn't attend every night, but I managed to support the Friday service and was happy to do so. But during choir rehearsal following the crusade, Minister Peoples expressed his disappointment regarding the choir's lack of attendance.

I took offense at his statement that such behavior showed the members' lack of commitment to the ministry. I realized there is no appreciation for members who make numerous sacrifices with a choir. Therefore, I withdrew my membership silently, having no hard feelings, but I really was disappointed and feeling unappreciated after years of dedication. Although I had been a member for a little over two years, I don't think Minister Peoples said over two hundred words to me during my entire membership.

Discouragement seems to surface later, when you're looking in your closet for something to wear, noticing clothing behind your weekly regulars. From choir robes to uniformed garments, colorful shirts and ties, as well as other accessories purchased in support of your participation. What's bad is that you can't wear those clothes just anywhere, only to the choir events, which they are in conjunction. So you have to wait until you're out of town to get a good wearing out of some of those clothes. God help you if you bumped into someone who had seen your choir somewhere and you were wearing a particular outfit; that would be embarrassing! I never was able to tell Minister Peoples thank you for the experience, but as of this day, I do appreciate him for allowing community singers from The Bronx to join his music ministry to express worship and praise to God.

About a year later I gathered three singers together and produced my own group! (I'm reluctant to give the name of the group because I heard the name is being used today.) Finding committed individuals focused on a similar goal is a great challenge when establishing a new group. I'm sure many ministry leaders have experienced the same challenges. But, Kenya Brodie, Lalisha McLean, and Kneesha Gill were the three singers who supported me during my first endeavor. I was committed to my goal but found others sometimes didn't grasp the same focus.

Naturally, I found myself using strategies learned while singing with Worship & Praise Mass Choir, having singers selling tickets and passing out flyers at numerous programs, with hopes of generating funding for an event. As of this day I'm not sure if my former singers felt unappreciated or used. Many believed I'd failed at my endeavors because we weren't a program-to-program or recording group. The total experience launched me into something I had no idea was ahead! (This chapter isn't meant to be autobiographical; therefore I can't itemize every aspect of my life and career.)

THE PRICE TAG

After this experience, a friend of mine called, asking if I could help her with a gospel musical called *All Things Are Possible,* (written and directed by Patricia Reeves for Pat Reeves Productions). Because I had worked with Pat Reeves from Worship & Praise Mass Choir and because she had helped me during one of my events, I didn't hesitate to say yes. When people launch new endeavors, they usually need help. Just as someone helped me during my initial steps, I was willing to help someone else.

As of this day, we're still doing the same for each other; I believe this in an act of sowing! But I don't want to get ahead of myself.... During the production I continued to learn other aspects of ministry, which now involved stage plays. I wasn't a lead actor or singer in the play (not sure why not), but I was committed to doing what was necessary. I must reiterate how imperative it is to focus only on being committed because there is really no compensation. Although I didn't expect any money, Pat Reeves graciously took the cast to dinner at a nice restaurant on Broadway!

For the next year I continued to launch endeavors that targeted business owners, including assisting my church home during a youth video recording. As months progressed, I began to feel burnt out after so much time spent planning, scheduling, and not really having finances to fund my desires. I felt trapped. I needed to find ways of earning money to fund another event. Many leaders experience similar issues when trying to formulate new endeavors, so how and where are they getting money?

1.3 LOS ANGELES

My next worship and fellowship experiences were in Los Angeles as a member of West Angeles COGIC (Church of God in Christ). My pastor Bishop Charles E. Blake was a confident man. A seemingly strong businessman and passionate ministry leader, I've never had a pastor, which nurtured his congregation as if we were everything that God had called us to be! For the first time in my life, I expressed feelings of how much I loved my church.

I've grown tremendously as a believer and even while I'm writing this today, I can't think of a time when leadership ever pressured or insulted us into supporting the ministry. We were taught the Word, encouraged to apply it to our lives, and that was it. It was up to us as congregants to live in obedience or disobedience to the Word. Even when it was in disobedience, I can't think of a time when there was any pressure, but just a loving message that encouraged us to make decisions to live in obedience. I believe that is the hope of many pastors, that congregants would rightly apply the Word to their lives, making sound decisions and growing prosperous as believers in Christ Jesus.

I wasn't actively a part of any of the ministry auxiliaries because of my previous involvements when in New York. I felt my new beginning in Los Angeles was a time for me to invest in what I wanted for me! I was no longer interested in ripping and running to support another ministry. Therefore, I wasn't someone you would know by name in the church. I was just a congregant that regularly attended and supported from my capacity. I tithed, as I should, although occasionally robbing God of the tithe when circumstances appeared. Still, I tried to maintain my commitment as best I could. I knew this ministry was good ground, and I knew I had to encourage myself to remain faithful!

THE PRICE TAG

I remember Bishop Blake at times asking if we could give twenty dollars during offering, but this was for the new cathedral construction. I had no problem with giving because the ministry never harassed the people. There wasn't any doubt this ministry was about nothing else but Kingdom building! For the first time in my life, I made a pledge toward a new cathedral, and I haven't completed it. Although I'm no longer a member of West Angeles, I'm still planning to complete that pledge because I still believe in the initial purpose of why I pledged.

As of this day, I haven't been able to find another church like West Angeles; the ministry is unique and I know there are hundreds of thousands of present and former members who would say the same. I will tell you more about my experience at West Angeles, later in the book. I have to outline my church relations so that you'll better understand my voice as a congregant, as well as the relevancy to the message in this book. I will deliberate on a variety of controversial subject matters.

While a member at West Angeles, I fellowshipped with Greater Bethany Community Church, now called the City of Refuge Church; Bishop Noel Jones is pastor. Although my obligation was at West Angeles, I didn't confuse my fellowship with this ministry. Just as many congregants maintain a fellowship with other ministries, I was the same. But there was that *dirty dishes* maxim planted in my mind years ago.

When evaluating what believers look for in a pastor, Bishop Noel Jones would be proven dynamic. His character exemplifies a profound foundation, demonstrating characteristics of our biblical leaders, even Christ Jesus. I know I shouldn't spotlight anyone in this book, but when God sends us a unique mouthpiece, you have to make known what's relevant from the Kingdom of God. Although today's focus is on the commercial pastor appeal,

Bishop Jones is our brother who shares from his heart the real beat of life that touches us in whatever situations we may face. Thank you, Jesus, for releasing a powerful man as such in the earth!

While fellowshipping with this ministry, I remember occasions when Bishop Jones would take money out of his own pocket and give it to congregants so that they would have something to give during offering. He clearly demonstrated how offering/giving was as equivalent to praising God (as when the choir is singing.) I never saw Bishop Jones conduct money or prophecy lines trying to obtain an offering, but only asked if the people could give if there was ever a need. (More on money and prophecy lines later.) Unlike some ministers who tend to change robes when away from home, I observed him carrying the same Christ-like characteristics into other ministries. Bishop Jones is a great example for early pastors and leaders who want to grow and excel their ministries. He clearly demonstrates the meekness, gentleness, and masculinity of Christ that congregations are seriously lacking!

One Sunday afternoon, while leaving service at West Angeles, I retrieved a flyer from a woman outside the church regarding an audition for a gospel musical called *Why Daddy? Why?* (written and directed by Ronda Morris for Virtuous Entertainment). Maintaining a career in media and entertainment, I was reluctant to begin participating in a gospel production. I can't recollect why, but I seemed to have penciled the audition date and attended. I arrived one Saturday afternoon to find hundreds of people, your typical cattle call. I was contemplating leaving because there were just too many people. Nevertheless, I began rehearsing my side (a portion of a character's script) and waited my turn to audition.

I received a callback a few days later, asking to return for a second audition. I was shocked they would consider me because my audition presentation was lazy; I was there for hours and became hungry! A few days later I traveled to Inglewood, California, on a Sunday afternoon, pulling up to someone's house for the callback. There weren't as many people as the week before, but there was still a crowd in and out of the house. I was really wondering what in the world I had gotten myself into.

I began combing the room for competition, observing there wasn't much as mainly older males were auditioning for the same role. When it was my turn, I felt the need to show off. I'm trained not to warm up to people but to step up ready to deliver what people want to ultimately see. I know what the saints like and that's what I gave them!

On the following evening I received a call from Ronda Morris asking if I would accept the role. She explained some aspects of the agreement process and asked if I could return, signing some paper work, retrieving the script, including meeting the selected cast. The selected cast arrived on a Friday night as packages were handed out to us along with a script. We had to sign documentation in order to receive the script, which included a contract that detailed "contingency pay." Cast members were confused in regards to what contingency pay meant, so Ronda began further explaining the motive behind the agreement. She explained that if the show made a profit, there would be opportunity for cast members to receive pay! But if it didn't, Virtuous Entertainment had no obligation to compensate the cast in any way and wouldn't be held responsible.

She continued explaining that if the show did make a substantial profit, the agreement still protected the ministry from cast members requesting any kind of compensation whatsoever. In other words, the ministry retained the right to use the cast to make money and not to pay anyone if they didn't want to. It also detailed that no compensation should be expected from cast contributions made toward the script, show and production.

Either way, it protected the ministry if profits were several thousands or a few dollars.

I've later discovered that most of the cast was from Faithful Central Bible Church; Bishop Kenneth C. Ulmer is pastor, which Ronda Morris attended. Therefore, many believed she would compensate the cast when the show made a profit, because we all believed the show would do well. I guess when you're in a Christian environment, dealing with individuals from church, you automatically assume believers possess Christ-like characteristics as your fellow brothers and sisters. Repeatedly we're taught about fellowship and how to greet and embrace other believers. But the day has changed; there is a strange vibe now in our congregations. Individuals now rehearse what we've known for years as the *Fellowship of the Saints*. It's becoming challenging to know who to trust in our assemblies!

Being involved in other areas of entertainment outside of ministry, I agreed to the terms, regarding it didn't conflict with my other interests. After several years of non-participation in ministry, I thought it would be a good idea to serve in some capacity. I remember discussing the details of this production with an industry friend and was warned, not to proceed with the agreement. But I considered all aspects and decided to proceed regardless, because I spent several years pursuing my own desires, in which at the time I thought it would be a good idea to participate.

Rehearsals began weekly on Friday nights, resuming on Saturday mornings for about three to fours hours. There were rehearsals schedules and targets given so the cast would be well rehearsed and polished for production. Later, members began showing up late and even not at all; therefore, Ronda began to lecture the cast about being responsible. She explained how there was an investor attached to the production, and she really wanted the cast to work hard and present a strong show, fearing the lost of capital invested.

THE PRICE TAG

This refocused the cast, as we were now aware that there was some kind of funding backing this venture. Many were now responsible, relating the seriousness regarding the potential lost of capital investment.

Not too long after, members began to slip again in their responsibilities. Lateness became typical, as many stopped at home to eat before coming to rehearsal on Friday evenings. Saturday mornings some chose to sleep a little late. On many occasions cast members weren't able to rehearse their scenes with the director because others required more attention. Realizing this was the first production for some cast members and they required additional time for coaching. It wasn't until I'd noticed some damaging un-professionalism from leadership that I began to get nervous about how far this production would go.

I was just a regular cast member who came to rehearsals to meet my obligations and leave. No one really knew anything about my background from New York or my current pursuits in Los Angeles because I didn't share anything with fellow cast members. I've learned through the years to do what you have to do and keep moving! Being in church for most of life, I've experienced folks getting all in your business, spreading it around and twisting it up as they're telling it. So I kept to myself therefore nothing negative could approach.

Not having a major role in the show, but a specific and identifying one, I wasn't someone that needed much attention at rehearsals. My character didn't have much involvement within the primary storyline; therefore, I didn't have to spend hours trying to block or rehearse a scene. There were times when I did my scene and was ready to leave for the day because I knew we weren't going to rehearse it again. Ronda later addressed the cast as to how faithful I was, how I arrived prepared, pre-rehearsed and doing a good job with my character. She used my work ethics as a demonstration to what was expected from other cast members. Her acknowledgement spotlighted me to the cast regarding I was someone that didn't say much and just participated from my capacity.

One Friday, we didn't rehearse for the entire evening as Ronda sat the cast down for discussion. One by one, we were asked to share how this production affected our lives personally. I instantly became nervous because this appeared to be a moment to bond with the cast. I honestly wasn't interested in that; I personally desired other things in my life and career and knew this production wasn't going to meet that desire. I just wanted to meet my responsibility and get it over with.

Each cast member began sharing how the message of the script had become an instrumental piece of work in his or her life. Several members of the cast shared personal experiences that it appeared Ronda already knew; casting them would create a stronger production. One of the stars of the show (S. Sambrano), around which the storyline of the script was surrounded, began to share with the cast her recent separation from her husband and financial hardship. She said that her brakes on her car were going bad and she didn't have any money to replace them. She explained that recent rehearsal scheduling had added additional wear and tear on her car. Everyone immediately became sympathetic, not knowing what to say, as we've all made some kind of sacrifice and probably had something pending in our lives as well. But the next few moments of her story clearly identified the kind of environment to which I had attached myself.

I remember Ronda stating, "We'll be praying for you," as I looked at this cast member crying because she earnestly needed help. (If I'm not mistaken, I believed we prayed for her at that moment.)

THE PRICE TAG

I wondered why leadership didn't just give her money to get her brakes replaced, as she was the star of the show. If she didn't have transportation to get back and forth to rehearsals, that would hinder the cast and definitely the progression for production, creating operational risk. Why is it that when folks need help, the religious thing to say is we'll be praying? I didn't think her need was a major situation that required thousands of dollars; in fact, I think she stated that she only needed three hundred dollars! By that time, we all knew that there was some kind of financial backing; therefore, there should have been some kind of support for such situations, even if it came directly out of the pocketbooks of leadership!

Well, I grew nervous, as it was now my turn to share with the cast. I began sharing how "I don't know why I'm here because I would rather be doing something else." I knew this was shocking because I was doing such a good job. I remember Ronda saying that she hoped I don't remove myself from the cast because my role was of importance to the show, as it was designed to really minister to the audience. I felt bad sharing real feelings, as (J. Pass) interjecting, "God having a purpose for all of us through this experience." That is always the religious thing to say, and I wasn't in acceptance. I shared what I was honestly feeling and it was now out-there for the folks to know.

These feelings developed as I began to notice similar situations as in New York: ripping and running (over-obligated), spending your own money, investing time to make someone else a profit, possibly walking away with nothing. I was now too involved to subtract my participation; cast members even began trying to encourage me to continue being faithful, as some really enjoyed my work, mentioning how it encouraged them as newcomers in theatre. But I still felt as if I had made a bad decision. It increasingly became a struggle, as I felt I was contributing so much energy that I could be using toward my own career goals. This was the warning I was given in the very beginning for an industry friend.

During this time of my life, I was experiencing financial challenges as well. I was young, living above my means and in "The Biz" full time; therefore, I had to work hard to meet all of my financial responsibilities. When you're working while experiencing challenges of your own, it immediately makes you aware of what you're doing for someone else. When forecasting the capacity of hardship that could approach, I had to try to understand how I was going to make additional money. This made the entire contingency agreement unattractive.

As I began to wrap up my personal thoughts, I told the cast member needing help that I would give her half the money needed for her brakes. If I would give half, I was pretty sure leadership or others would contribute to the other half. (I'm still not sure if leadership and other cast members contributed anything.) She was so grateful that someone in the cast would help her, but in my head, I was still confused why leadership didn't support her need, as she was the lead actress of the show. This was another opportunity for me to understand how there is no appreciation for those who make continual sacrifices to help someone else! I also began to see how ministries have a set structure established to make money from others, supplying no help for even their own who support them. Look what happens to the faithful!

If that wasn't more than enough reasons to make an exit, things became worse as months progressed. Cast members continually grew irresponsible, making excuses that slowed down progress. Leadership didn't seem to realize that when people are doing something for free, they don't have the same mindset as if they were being paid. Leadership began to become stern regarding these changes, as some cast members began reflecting the same attitude about the environment. Rehearsal after rehearsal there were problems because folks were starting to get frustrated and worn out (physically drained), trying to keep up with something that wasn't paying their bills or putting food on their tables!

Of course you can't speak up or talk back while leadership is trying to flex a muscle regarding dedication issues, as it's always popular for them to use our commitment as an example of how Christ is committed to us. That's verbal abuse if you ask me. Why does leadership always throw the Bible at us when they're trying to control the people? Scripture after Scripture, leadership tried to beat the people trying to obtain control and order. Breaking down in tears and using dramatization to display anger and frustration, leadership continued to use several scenarios to motivate or discipline the cast. This seemed to have become a typical Friday night special, as leadership seemed prepared to demonstrate their authority!

If you've dared to get in the way, you would have been replaced or asked to leave. And we all know someone has to be made an example as a way of demonstrating authority! Cast members had committed so much of their time by this point that it would have been silly to walk away. These weekly episodes didn't motivate cast members but only ushered fear into the environment. We all were trying, but many times our ministry leaders become so detached from the real feelings of their supporters that they couldn't see how folks were burnt out from discouragement!

As crunch time grew nearer, the environment turned hostile. More rehearsal demands, obligations, and dramatization from leadership caused some cast members to become stubborn...and I was one of them. I was so tired of doing the right thing and still collectively feeling harassed and trying not to take outbursts personally; but after a while, you begin taking offense because we're all in this together! There was no more motivation; folks were just pressed to do this and do that because this is what God was allegedly calling for.

Members were seemingly becoming obstacles as leadership clearly was failing in their sensitivity toward individual concerns. Therefore, as a fellow cast member, I stepped in to try to motivate the people. On every Friday evening before rehearsal, I stopped by Pizza Hut and ordered about four medium pies, so cast members could come straight from work knowing there was food and drinks. Even on Saturday mornings, I stopped by Winchell's Donuts and purchased about two-dozen donuts and juice, motivating cast members to be on time. Experiencing challenges of my own, but mainly from my own pocket for nearly an entire month, I began to feed the cast on a weekly basis. This had now become the second but not final time in which I had to reach into my pocket to support this ministry, all the while working on a contingency basis!

Feeding the cast had clearly begun to motivate members, as some caught on to what I was doing and started bringing coffee and other things in support of motivation. I will never forget the voice of (Debbie Kay Smith), the main star of the show, stating, "All I want is a cup of coffee!" For weeks, continually making mention of her one desire, no one had caught on to what she was asking. You would have thought this act of kindness would have motivated leadership to even say thank you.

I've learned from this experience that whenever you step in to do what leadership is not doing, you cause a shifting within a ministry. In other words, people will begin to shift their attention in the direction of the one that is giving! God's people are delicate; we're so fragile, needing compassionate leadership. So when we're feeling misled or mistreated, we walk off or shift to the place(s) where

THE PRICE TAG

we're getting what we need. That's why many congregants move from church to church and ministry to ministry!

The leadership of this ministry now observed me as someone to be *behind the vision* (in support of the ministry). He's taking money out of his own pocket to support, so this must mean we can use him to get other stuff done. This production was in serious trouble! They thought things were going well, but it was really suffering.

There was also an occasion when we were asked to go to Six Flags Magic Mountain to promote the show at a yearly gospel event held in the park. The cast was asked to pay twenty dollars, which covered admission. I was reluctant to attend; at that point I wasn't interested in becoming part of a street team for promotions. I remember receiving a phone call from (Allison Webb), another ministry leader, regarding me being the only cast member not attending. I felt bad hearing this, as it made me look like I wasn't being supportive. I'm entitled to make a decision whether I support anything, but for some reason ministries make us continually feel as if we have no choice!

Still, I went, and the entire cast carpooled to the event. We were all handed a huge stack of flyers for promotional purposes. I observed cast members and even the stars of the show putting them in their bags, going off to enjoy a fun-filled day at the amusement park! That wasn't the motive for our attending. As hundreds of people every few hours attended this gospel event without flyers in their hands, I knew we were in even more trouble! I asked a security guard if I could come into the amphitheatre to pass out flyers before the next event started in order to get them in the hands of the people. I had to pass out flyers in this big amphitheatre alone, while my fellow cast members were enjoying themselves on the rides. I remember later feeling so disgusted with the ministry, feeling that the show wasn't going to do well at all.

At this point leadership began to notice me as someone who could be very instrumental, whereas I'd previously displayed skill sets for other areas of production! Isn't that how it always works? Once leadership finds out you can do more than expected, they begin to plot how they can use you even more. Well, I had attached myself to that environment: passing out flyers at events, hanging up posters around town, and even driving to San Diego trying to add additional cities to the show. Week by week, there was always something that needed to be done!

Once you begin to understand the behind-the-scenes dealings of what ministries have to do, your focus can sometimes change. I can recall there being other individuals associated with leadership, in which I'm not sure if they were doing much of anything. I'm not sure what amount of capital was invested into the production, but it sure wasn't enough to cover many of the necessities. Cast members were solicited to sell advertising opportunities to businesses and individuals desiring display advertising in the show's program. After all the other time consuming endeavors, this was the last thing I was interested in doing! There was no way I was now going to become a salesman, trying to sell advertising opportunity. I believe we were given a quota of one hundred dollars. I just wrote a check for one hundred dollars because at that point I didn't want anyone calling my home regarding not selling anything!

Let me remind you once again that all of the dedication members were continually showing fell under terms of contingency pay. It should appear that leadership was now requesting so much of members' time and finances that we were forgetting about the clauses in the agreement stating (paraphrased), "We should not expect any compensation for contributions made to the script and/or production." Leadership has a way of getting you so wrapped up into trying to meet the alleged purpose/will of God that

THE PRICE TAG

we disregard many areas not using wisdom! Therefore, after you're all used up, broke, frustrated and discouraged, they then throw in your face how you should have used wisdom in the first place!

That's when folks get mad and want to start acting ugly because they then feel manipulated, robbed and scammed! You believe you're doing what is necessary unto the Lord, but really helping someone else with their finances! Well, I must tell you, things became very ugly between me and the leadership of this ministry! By the end of just a six-month agreement, I've additionally paid for an original song for myself in the show to increase the number of original selections for production, including submitted plans for a national tour. Toward the end of the liquidation of my contract, I was accused of trying to steal her show, including getting money from the box office.

These kinds of accusations caused leadership and I to begin acting like sinners (un-repented). Cast members desired to physically fight me, as many of them were from the same church and taking up for each other; production supporters harassed me while leadership called my house with threats and a host of other plots trying to initiate fear! (I remember my microphone dropping dead in the middle of my scene during a sold-out Friday night performance. I had to yell so surrounding microphones could pick up my voice).

After continual adversity between leadership and myself, I knew they weren't going to pay me for my participation. Although working under contingency pay, I knew at this point that leadership would use the signed documentation against me; therefore, I was expecting nothing! The show without question had made a profit, whereas Virtuous Entertainment was able to pay members, but no one called me regarding compensation.

A few days later, while having a conversation with a fellow member of the cast, I was informed that members were picking up their checks at a cast party. I was upset that leadership didn't call me directly to invite me to the party or mention that we would receive pay at that time. I called Ronda several times, leaving messages as I felt I was being ignored. But one evening I did receive a return phone call from her stating that I could pick up a check at the cast party. I declined to attend, as I was no longer interested in being involved in any further endeavors of the ministry. As I was trying to figure out an alternative, she explained that it would be best that I attend. As I continued to decline the invitation, a comment was replied regarding me being scared as to no one at the party was going to hurt me! (Let me remind you that these are Christians operating a ministry.)

I wanted to collect what was due because I'd invested six months of my time and was dedicated until the end. So I called Ronda again a few days later to ask about retrieving the check. (Isn't it a shame that you work so diligently for folks, but then when it's time to get paid, you have to get ugly?) After no return calls for several days, I began to have some nasty feelings about her. I was upset that I'd invested six months of my time, just to be ignored by someone for whom I'd made money!

I later received a message from Ronda stating, "The check is in the mail!" (We've all heard this junk before.) I replied to the message, stating, "I've worked in your face; I rather be paid in my hand." Arrangements were later made for me to pick up my check at Allison's Webb House. I traveled to Allison's home with a relative of mine as a witness in case of any foul play. Ronda and Allison were there as I was handed a check without an envelope. I felt this behavior was another indication of being unprofessional, and I proceeded to ask for an envelope, all the while keeping conversation

THE PRICE TAG

to a minimum, trying to not get into any further verbal disputing. As I said thank you and preceded to leave the house, it appeared Ronda and Allison were prepared for further adversity. But since I had a relative with me, it would have been out of place and disrespectful. After all the threats and hostility between us, I wasn't stupid enough to show up at a woman's house alone, especially while trying to retrieve money! (Imagine how that would have played out in front of a Los Angeles judge.)

That was the last time I ever saw Ronda Morris and Allison Webb. The closure of our fellowship was complete as I signed my agreement in that house and picked up my contingency pay. While leaving the neighborhood, I was curious as to how much the check was for. I should have looked while in the house, but the atmosphere was ready for further aggression. When I opened the envelope, I saw that the check was payable for only two hundred dollars! I was just as shocked as you are now, because I'd clearly put more money into the ministry than what was returned. I later found out that other cast members, even those with minimal involvement, were paid more! Well, the truth is, I'd signed and agreed to contingency pay, and that's what I've received. It was a challenge trying to move on with my life with only two hundred dollars after a six-month investment.

I guess Ronda and Allison were confident that I received what I deserved, until the *Los Angeles Times* hit the newsstands about two weeks later. I was shocked to receive a call from Ronda mentioning that I should pick up a copy of the paper. I did. It featured a lengthy article regarding three shows that had a successful run in Los Angeles. While reading the beginning of the article, I was looking for some kind of reference to why she wanted me to pick up the paper. It wasn't until I turned the page that I observed a half page picture of guess who. That's right, me! I was completely shocked that I would have a photo in this big newspaper! I couldn't compare to the real stars of the show, nor did my character have continuous scripting with the storyline. Out of all the scenes that were photo worthy, why mine? Remember the Friday night performance when my microphone went dead in the middle of my scene? Well, that's the same night the photojournalist captured the picture! (I had no microphone in my hand.)

The article was lengthy, as it did cover other productions, but I was still shocked that not one time did they mention Ronda Morris's name as playwright or director! I guess as of this day, when she pulls out her memorabilia reflecting back on her past work, there will always be a face she'll remember! I cashed the two hundred dollar check and then left Los Angeles nearly twenty-four hours later!

1.4 LAS VEGAS

Las Vegas had a totally different environment than New York and Los Angeles. Although the city is known for gaming and entertainment, it also has a church community. I guess with its stigma, many will need to find their way to the cross eventually. Finding a good church is the hardest thing any believer will ever have to experience! If you were the kind of person who has been a member of the same church for decades and never had to really look for another church home, then you wouldn't understand what I'm talking about. But there are thousands of believers changing churches every five to ten years, even sooner sometimes. Everyone has his or her own reason, but most of the time it's because individuals are finding themselves stuck, unfulfilled, confused, or upset about something specific.

THE PRICE TAG

I began to fellowship with a few churches in Las Vegas over the years but I wasn't interested in joining another ministry. The last ministry I was part of was COGIC, so I tried other COGIC churches in hopes of finding a good fit. Most people believe it doesn't matter what kind of church you attend, that if it's a place of worship there is no reason to be selective. As much as I've traveled, I'll tell you firsthand that it does matter what kind of ministry you attach yourself to because of doctrines and so many other things dominating churches. We all have to be reminded that God has called some people to the Gospel, while others have entered with their own motives. You'll spend years trying to figure things out, all the while becoming frustrated because the environment severely turns hostile and controlling.

From church to church I was unsuccessful in locating a ministry I felt was a good fit. I know you're wondering why didn't I just pray and allow the Holy Spirit to lead me somewhere. Most likely, I was probably led somewhere, but I didn't stay long enough understanding His purpose! So for the first time in my life, I've become a believer without a home church. We all know how bad this sounds, and many would throw Scripture regarding forsaking the assembling of the saints. Until you're in a situation in which you have to relocate and find a new church, you'll never understand how in a land full of ministries, few are really serving!

I grew accustomed to listening and watching radio and television every Sunday. Radio ministries are unique in that some would have 15-30 minutes time slots and others even had 45 minutes in an hour! KCEP 88.1 FM would play gospel music starting early on Sunday mornings, and there would be preaching and teaching following, then resuming gospel music for most of the day. Even during the midweek, there would be gospel music all day on Wednesdays. I must tell you, you can experience good church right at home, no matter what some might say. There is no distraction, no touching your neighbor every three minutes, and all that other junk that now filters our congregations these days. I'm not mentioning this to justify staying home to enjoy broadcasted ministries, but to share my voice as a congregant.

When Prophetess Amanda Irving from Moments of Miracles Deliverance Church came on the air for just 15 minutes, you were sure to hear something that was going to stir you up. Prophetess Irving was a voice much needed in Las Vegas. She was probably the only person I've heard in my life that was bold enough in her faith to speak in tongues on the air. She didn't hold back her belief and would declare the Word of God with boldness. (I've recently heard she is no longer on the air, as she has been challenged by a stroke.) If you didn't attend church, Prophetess Irving would stir the radio waves in such a powerful way, that you would be behind closed doors with uplifted hands and talking back at the radio. I truly believed people even tuned in while driving to their particular churches because she was such a relevant voice from God who delivered with confidence and determination.

The Sunday morning radio strip continued with a woman by the name of Prophetess Glories Powell from The Moment of Truth Ministries. (Have you noticed how everyone's title is now Bishop, Prophet or Prophetess? I'm going to leave that alone for now.) Prophetess Powell was such an inspiration, delivering the Word of God with such a loving and compassionate voice! After Prophetess Irving had heated up the radio waves, loosing and binding everything, Glories furthered the Gospel with compassion and gentleness in her voice. Following the week of September 11, 2001, Prophetess Powell spoke the most life-changing Word I've ever heard. As of this day, I still share my experience about how it instantaneously changed my perception of how I view God the

Father. Having Prophetess Irving and Powell on the air on Sunday, I became content with enjoying the Word at home. For a few years it was my regular routine.

One day while listening to the radio I heard that Bishop Noel Jones was coming to town to minister at a church called Mountaintop Faith Ministries, where Bishop Clinton House is Senior Pastor. I remember wondering why I hadn't heard of the church before, for if Bishop Jones fellowshipped with this ministry; it must be a good church. Mountaintop Faith Ministries was a progressive church, full of young people growing and enjoying their salvation! It seemed to be a fast-growing ministry, as many people were leaving other churches and attaching themselves to this one. To my knowledge, it was a peaceful church with an established warm-spirited environment, and believers were able to move immediately into the flow of the House. I began to fellowship on occasion, but I still wasn't interested in joining another church. Because of its reputation and the overall spirit of the House, I believe this ministry is going to do great things. I've even referred individuals to this ministry, because of the amount of time and effort it takes to locate a good church. I pray God's continual blessing upon this House and leadership because Las Vegas needs such a ministry.

In addition to my fellowship with church ministries, I've had some involvements with outreach endeavors in gospel music. A former company of mine (BESO International) began producing national tours. We received a proposal to tour a gospel concert featuring known recording artists. I approached it as if I were producing a show for a non-gospel artist; I submitted plans for the best! As things progressed, situations grew continually frustrating. While dealing with managers and agents of many artists, I discovered that there is limited opportunity for gospel artists outside of the convention and sanctuary arenas. I remember receiving phone calls from booking agents seeking to get their artists on particular tours. I was puzzled, wondering how they even knew we existed. I've discovered that everybody knows everybody. Once you hang up the phone with one person, they would speed dial someone else to spread the news around.

I learned that the gospel music industry has many problems. I've felt there are many people hiding behind the word *Gospel*, when they really want what the Church calls the *secular!* From lying managers and agents to overpriced and demanding artists, I'd began learning that behind all the outward appearance were situations that were a complete turn off. This isn't something people really want to hear about (Christian/gospel music or the Church), but it's now time to have a voice, letting people know that as God's people, dragging major situations throughout the decades!

I'd run into argumentative situations with managers and booking agents regarding the amount of money paid, but still choir members were not being paid! Remembering my own personal experiences, I would not be a part of paying those who are doing the same things as Virtuous Entertainment had done in Los Angeles! Many thought I was out of place to ask if choir members were paid, causing an uncomfortable environment during negotiations. How are ministry leaders pocketing all the money (only paying musicians, of course) and not giving singers anything? It's amazing how the names in front of the group (which most times can't sing ten notes on key) make all the money and the real singers take home nothing more but church punch, pound cake, and occasionally a stomach virus from food gone bad! (read Section 5.1)

During the last two years of my residency in Las Vegas, I became accustomed to watching the Trinity Broadcasting Network (TBN). On Sundays I found myself watching for hours, spending most of

THE PRICE TAG

the day in front of the television. TBN offered a variety of Christian programming, and believers could find several types of teaching and preaching ministries!

Watching TBN began to open my eyes regarding many aspects of televised evangelism. I found myself emotionally shifting from program to program. What I'm trying to communicate is that ministries structure their programs to attract your attention and then begin solicitation. It was almost like a sales presentation that detailed many aspects of a product or service, and then hit you with the price at the end!

Twice a year TBN has a *praise-a-thon* to financially support the network. I remember calling one day to give a "one-time gift." I must tell you that there is no such thing as a one-time gift because TBN began flooding my mailbox with envelopes for continual giving. I then realized I should have never given my personal information over the phone. I should have just mailed some money, with no return address on the envelope, to the address on the screen. We'll talk more about this later in the book!

1.5 ATLANTA

Atlanta, Georgia was a well-needed change in my life, and I began to make decisions regarding how I chose to worship! I'd discovered that after a few years of enjoying the comforts of broadcasted ministries that my life lacked the interaction with other believers. I knew the established atmosphere of sanctuary worship was essential, as I was not involved in corporate prayer, impartation and other aspects of sanctuary worship. These decisions were caused by several areas of ministry many try to stay far away from!

Needing restoration in my life, including other transitional particulars of my personal life, I sought the Lord for change. I began my fellowship routine, which allowed me to attend any particular church in hopes of possibly attaching myself to a ministry. Fellowshipping with other ministries wasn't easy, as churches were becoming aggressive, even harassing their visitors. It's no wonder that many people choose not to attend every Sunday because sanctuary officials are now walking the aisles looking for unfamiliar faces! Once I personally feel harassed, I typically leave the ministry. If they don't allow visitors the opportunity to attend without pressure, that's not the place for me!

Many ministries are now structuring their alter calls to aggressively pursue new members. They actually ask you to encourage and solicit neighbors without a home church to join the assembly. If you're fellowshipping with a church on a weekly basis, you have to either decline the invitation weekly or stop attending, because you're not ready to make a decision. Although many congregants are pressured to join, there are always those who never return or rarely attend.

Having the exposure to TBN allowed me the opportunity to attend two churches I'd only seen on television. I visited World Changers Church International, where Dr. Creflo A. Dollar is pastor. Dr. Creflo A. Dollar Ministries (from the Changing Your World broadcast) was a tremendous blessing in my life. You must understand that watching television is different from attending the actual church. Television doesn't permit viewers the opportunity to capture the full scope of a particular ministry. I call it the cut-and-paste method. Televised programs have nearly twenty minutes to deliver the Word before hitting viewers with product offers during the remaining time.

THE PRICE TAG

The actual congregation seemed to be mature, as the demographics appeared older. I had a concern when looking across the sanctuary noticing few individuals in my age range; later discovering there was a separate service for the youth. I didn't attend every Sunday, as I found the pace of the ministry very slow. I felt as if I were back in school, looking for an excuse to raise my hand to retrieve a bathroom pass to walk the halls! I kept telling myself that I should remain focused; as I was trying to condition myself back to being among a fellowship at least twice a week. I continued to grow weary, finding the doctrine repetitious, but there were also several others aspects of the ministry that I knew I had to talk to someone about.

When watching on television, thirty minutes is seemingly quick and to the point, but when actually attending the church, I found myself bored and flipping through tons of Scriptures receiving new definition or personalized interpretation! The doctrine appeared to be a reverse of what I'd been learning for years; references were even made that congregants had wrong interpretations. It was almost like learning the Bible all over again; there was always something wrong with what the congregants already believed! Sometimes I thought Dr. Dollar was trying to communicate that the translated Bible had been screwed up in the process.

Now many teachers such as Dr. Dollar have to structure their ministries in ways wherefore congregants can really understand interpretations. Regarding many congregants have changed ministries not once but a few times, it's evident you'll find believers that are taught differently; therefore pastors are now restructuring their new member classes and other type sessions teaching the belief system of the House. I found the belief system process at this ministry too long and very tiresome, probably because of my prior experiences with other ministries.

World Changers Church began to open my eyes to some changes that now infiltrate many ministries because televised ministries are now trendsetters to others. Before members were able to return Tithes and offering, leadership would provoke this time of worship by asking the congregation, "Are there any millionaires in the House?" It was now congregants' moment for prosperity; as this question would bring forth a loud cheer as congregants waved their offerings in the air! I guess this was an act of faith toward the direction of being prosperous. I found this to become annoying week after week, service after service. I began to believe it was almost like selling a false hope to many that desired money! Congregants were then asked to be silent, which was their personal time to hear the Holy Spirit revealing how much money they should give during the offering! I was puzzled as to how I could hear from the Holy Spirit in only fifteen seconds about how much I should give during offering. I thought it was definitely deceptive because I know for sure that not all congregants are that in tune with the Holy Spirit! If we are, or rather, if the World Changers congregation is, how is it, that's the only time in a seven-day period when we're able to hear clearly from the Holy Spirit when requesting instruction? Why can't we do this Monday through Saturday? Why can't we connect that quickly when we're eating all the wrongs foods, knowing that we could be overweight? Why can't we hear from the Holy Spirit that quickly during temptation, wrong decisions, and even how we're spending our money?

Our global society is growing compulsive; it languages more and more; bigger and bigger; and faster and faster, always demonstrating dissatisfaction! I felt the practice was doing just that. It fuels the compulsiveness of society, deceiving believers into thinking they're outdoing the world's way of thinking, not knowing they already possess the purchased possession which is the

Holy Ghost! Wouldn't the Holy Spirit clearly remind you of himself? But we're no longer disciplined to the Holy Spirit; we're now forced to believe if the Holy Spirit doesn't move the same way through leadership, it's not relevant to how it's moving in our lives! What I'm saying is that leadership is now becoming so controlling that they're essentially saying that if we want things to happen for us, we must first, make them happen for the House or leadership!

These types of statements then hinder the Holy Spirit within the life of the believer because now we're no longer able to recognize clear and specific direction regarding our lives. We're always checking to see if that's the same flow/moving with leadership. I'm not saying that a leader doesn't have instruction for the people, but controlling pastors and ministry leaders will make you feel as if your spirituality is only relevant when it's time to get something from you! (I apologize to all those in other countries that we reach by way of electronic communication, demonstrating these practices).

Scripture after Scripture, new interpretation after new interpretation, I found myself feeling excluded from the environment at World Changers Church. I wondered why I wasn't leaping with everyone else. Why wasn't I receiving while everyone else was receiving, I became annoyed, believing something was wrong or missing within me!

There were even times during the service, while everyone was getting excited, that I stood looking across the sanctuary, noticing I wasn't the only one not excited! What became so confusing was when people began to walk up to the pulpit, tossing their money on the stairs! It always starts with one or two idiots, and then it progresses to hundreds of other people doing the same thing. Immediately, I'm wondering why people are feeling the need to give a gratuity for the Word! Why would someone believe it's spiritual to walk to the front of a church and toss their money on the stairs? This is the compulsiveness I'm talking about! Individuals feel as if they have to pay for God's attention, pay for His provision, and even pay for the expediting of His grace or revealed glory! While it's customary to issue a gratuity to those who work in the service industry, the practice has now stormed our sanctuaries, as believers feel they need to tip men and women of God who delivers a particular Word!

Many restaurants today are adapting the automatic gratuity added to all guest tickets; therefore, patrons are no longer able to use their own judgment regarding the service they've received. Now, restaurant employees are able to supply any kind of service because their gratuities are automatically generated, it's becoming the same with church today. Many congregants feel as if they no longer have a choice regarding how to support a ministry; some even tell you exactly how much money they want you to give. Although congregants still retain the choice of whether to give, leaders use tactics to persuade us, making us feel guilty if not giving what is being asked. I haven't personally witnessed Dr. Dollar asking for a specific amount of money during offering, causing many to proceed to approach the altar. It seems as if a trend has now begun, as this practice seems to follow Dr. Dollar as he travels to other ministries. Once you begin to televise certain aspects of what people are doing in a local assembly, others watching may feel the need to do the same thing, believing it's a new move of the Holy Ghost. This practice has now spilled into other ministries and congregants are tipping the clergy for the Word of God!

I was complete annoyed while attending Manpower 2003 (TD Jakes Ministries). As Dr. Dollar was invited to minister, thousands of people felt the need to leave their seats to throw money on the stairs in a crowded arena, causing so much commotion. There was no way thousands of people were able to approach the altar of this arena, let alone make their way back to their seats. Therefore, believers felt the need to crumble up their money and throw it as far as possible! Do you believe this foolishness? Why would someone feel the need to crumble up an offering and throw it? I was almost irate, believing leadership should have rebuked the House!

It was clear that congregants have forgotten why we bring an offering and how to represent our gifts in worship unto the Lord! What is one really thinking when he/she feels the need to crumble up his/her offering and throw it? Is that how we now represent our worship? What if God crumbled up your provision and threw it so you had to go out of your way to get it? So, how do you think the Father feels when we offer lazy and/or unorthodox worship in His presence? You would think leadership would have stopped the service or have done something (besides smile at the people) to remind congregants how we present our offering to the Lord! But as long as the money was coming, it just appeared to be another powerful move by God! I guess we wouldn't know power, if we were all electrocuted at the same time!

This action took so much time, as officials had to sweep the money into big piles and take it in for processing. As Dr. Dollar continued to minister, interruption still came as occasionally something would hit you on the head! When you took the time to look at what hit you, it was more crumpled-up money that hadn't made its way to the front of the arena! It was time to play "Throw the Money." Several congregants began throwing crumbled up money, trying to get it up to the front of the arena. This was the most unethical thing I've ever seen in my life!

Bishop Jakes later addressed this issue (smiling with the people), mentioning how it takes so much time to unfold all of the money, placing it in the machines for calculation. (I was advised the same behavior had taken place the night before when Bishop Eddie L. Long ministered the Word; I didn't attend that service). I guess, when it comes to receiving money, no one would dare stop and demand order! I pray this practice doesn't continue to infiltrate other assemblies, as large conventions tend to be the training grounds for inspiring leaders seeking to implement strategies within their own ministries (read Section 3.4).

As I mentioned earlier, there were many occasions when I was blessed by Dr. Dollar's ministry, but there are several aspects of it, which I believe is out of control or structured to really get from the people having no refuge for those that really need! Yes, the ministry participates in outreach and does serve in areas of missions, but congregants have to afford these things on a continual basis. At present I don't support World Changers Church or Dr. Creflo A. Dollar Ministries, but during the summer of 2004 I did!

The ministry solicited the world to help its televised broadcasts, as it was a few million dollars in debt. I gave the thirty-five dollars that was asked because I know there are those who need and desire the Gospel in their homes. But I was still confused and growing annoyed by what pastors and leaders are doing putting their ministries in debt, and then turning around and saying, "Well, let's just get it from the people."

How is it that he could solicit the world for help and still continue to allegedly fly around in his private plane(s)? Why couldn't he offset some of his debt by flying commercially for the summer, knowing that's the season in which many ministries experience similar setbacks? Isn't that using wisdom with our finances? Can we afford to enjoy luxuries when our households are experiencing debt? Can we maintain luxuries while other responsibilities are failing? They preach about how we spend our money, but then they use our contributed finances in ways that sometimes sink the ministry in debt!

Where do congregants get money when we're experiencing debt? We have to max out our credit cards, live from paycheck to paycheck, avoid paying a particular bill to afford another, or get creative financially in order to survive. Unless we're on the streets, we can't solicit people to give us money, and we can't continue affording luxuries when in debt! Many times congregants give so much to the ministry that they have no money to make it to the next payday and have to live on noodles and canned tuna!

So does this mean that the next time Changing Your World Broadcast experiences debt, will we have to give again? Oh why not? The People helped before, why not again? How are we going to afford our local assemblies now that televised ministries are asking too? (read Section 4.1). Other ministry leaders observe these practices, which gives them a plan for when their ministry experiences debt!

Sooner or later, we'll have ministry associates showing up at our front doors asking for money! Dr. Creflo A. Dollar Ministries and TD Jakes Ministries are already telemarketing for money, phoning current and former supporters. It never stops! Once one of them rakes in millions with a strategy, the next is ready to execute it as well! We have to be very careful how we're supporting ministry these days. We as congregants are so sentimental and most times vulnerable, believing our good deeds are going to usher more of God's presence into our lives or have him treat us differently. Whether you've giving thirty thousand dollars or thirty cents, God knows what's in your heart!

The solution isn't for leadership to say, "Oh, we'll just get it from the people" every time there is a need. Maybe the ministry is operating above its means. Possibly the solution should be to downsize the financial capacity of the ministry, including the amount of programming syndicated? They're spending too much money trying to compete in the marketplace. Oh, you better believe it's a marketplace! There's big business and declining stewardship now affecting thousands of assemblies. (read Section 3.1).

I'm getting a little ahead of myself but it becomes offensive when pastors beat up their congregants about how we live above our means, when the ministry is doing the same thing! But the justification is that they're Kingdom Building. We will talk more about this later in the book.

I also witnessed another damaging situation, where there was a homeless married couple living out of their car! What was mind-blowing is that they were not just congregants attending a large ministry and nobody really knew them. They were members of a praise team! They told their story at Manpower 2003, knowing that God has intervened in their situation. But behind the story and testimony, there was something missing!

Leaders, (and I consider praise team singers to be leaders) serving within a multimillion-dollar ministry should NOT find themselves homeless; or in any ministry, come to think about it! I know what you're thinking: how can a ministry support thousands of unfortunate situations? But we're not talking about regular congregants here; we're talking praise team members, who are officially the front line, preparing the atmosphere for services so the Holy Spirit can do the work! So how in the world can these people have nobody to call? Why is there no protocol in place? There are designated phone numbers for people to call to give money; why can't there be a designated phone number for leaders and congregants to call when they need help? (I could be speculating, as I'm not sure if the ministry has such a phone number.)

THE PRICE TAG

The most disturbing aspect of these situations I will further discuss later in the book, but I must tell you that when you bring these kinds of situations to leadership's attention, they'll sometimes find a way to make it seem as if you're not doing the right things or applying principals correctly! They'll make you feel as if the sin in your life is always going to hold you down. Meanwhile, it's not sin, but the bondage that the ministry places on you. Then you begin to blame God for what is or is not happening in your life. We need to evaluate what we believe about the ministries we attend and how we support it!

There is also a part of service at World Changers Church called "Congregational Appeal." This is when a member is approved to stand in front of the congregation to solicit the people for help. If you needed money, food, shelter, or whatever, time would be set-aside for you to stand in the front of the church and humiliate yourself! When there are thousands of allegedly prosperous people staring in your face, how in the world can someone get up enough courage to stand before church folks asking for help?

I found this disturbing; it is difficult to understand why this portion of service even existed. If a congregant finds him or herself in a situation needing help, there should be some other protocol; perhaps members can meet with a ministry associate to obtain help! Because this kind of structure humiliates individuals, I'm sure there are many who really need help, but refuse to make their requests known. I'm not sure if his spiritual father in the Gospel has passed down this ministry tactic even other similar practices, but from my experiences, many people use what they know and work with what they've been taught! There is nobody to call when ministries have collectively found ways to use methods which are allegedly God's will placing congregants in situations that turn them off and eventually send us running away!

Large ministries will always have too many people to reach and never really an ear to hear concerns because the continual goals are always for further progression. The ministry can then ensure its profit and testify how God is really blessing them. But the truth is that there are hurting and discouraged people who have done much of the financing without even receiving a thank you! These situations will continue to flood our sanctuaries, as there are thousands of new ministries now structuring themselves to be just like the big ones! That means more goals, more forecasting and agendas, and more hurting congregants with no voice and nowhere to go!

Thousands of congregants are going to begin worshiping in the privacy of their homes. This is not what spiritual people desire, but we're recognizing that ministry leadership cannot play the same games with those who are seasoned! Many of us have been around the block a few times. We've helped build ministries, knowing the hard work and financial commitment it takes to support a vision. Pastors therefore have to concentrate on new naive members who believe that this is what they must do to show their commitment to the Lord! This cycle continues every five to seven years of a ministry. That's how many churches continue to sustain after hundreds have moved on. The House will shift again! What didn't work with you will work with the next flock!

How is it pastors become bold enough to actually tell us to leave? We are God's people and the sheep of His pasture; you can't turn us away! What kind of shepherd does that? Many times I've arrived home from a Sunday service thinking that we must be back in the days of atonement! Ministry leaders are making us feel that if they don't repent for us, we won't be forgiven; if they don't head to the mountain, we won't hear from God; if they don't lay hands on us, we won't be healed or made whole; and if we won't bring an offering, we won't be blessed but cursed!

1.5 BACK TO NEW YORK
(Familiar Place–Needing God's Grace)

Returning home to New York wasn't easy. Sometimes people feel this way about the places where they've grown up or lived before. I earnestly tried to keep the same focus as when I was in Atlanta, regarding remaining in fellowship. So I didn't want too much time to pass before finding a church I could attend regularly. I began attending Greater Faith Temple Deliverance Church (GFT), where Michelle White-Hayes is pastor.

This was the first time I fellowshipped with a ministry where a woman was pastor. I'm not implying ability of women to be pastors. My point is that the ministry had some areas that I found discouraging as a man! Unfortunately, there are a large number of women in authority within ministry and other business entities, consistently feeling the need to demonstrate the absence of men, in position interjecting statements, which immediately alliances women together creating an atmosphere demonstrating power. It's become common for many ministries to appeal to their largest constituency, which are women.

The environment that is associated with ministry seems to have a concept of Christianity having feminine roles. We're continually taught about the sentimental aspects of Jesus as being nurturing, gentle and very compassionate. These attributes tend to suffocate the masculinity of Christ. Due to an overwhelming number of leaders seeking to position their assemblies having these characteristics, men have begun taking a back seat feeling disenfranchised. This is clearly the wrong message, as ministries need to discover the masculinity of Jesus!

Although GFT is predominately women, there were statements and analogies used which possibly were offensive to male congregants; maybe that's why there were very few in attendance. Observing for several weeks the type of ministry I was now attending, I knew I had to use caution. I also found the structure of the ministry rather disconcerting, as congregants had to stand as Pastor Hayes entered the sanctuary, departed from the sanctuary, and even as she approached the pulpit. This isn't a unique design, as this happens in thousands of ministries. Throughout my life, I have found this annoying. I don't mind clapping in recognition of the authority over the House, but ministries are now controlling, regarding giving the man or woman of God too many accolades during the duration of even one service! Nowadays you can sometimes get a better response from having the people praise their pastor than when mentioning the name Jesus! The behavior seems to take away the focus of why we attend church. Praise and worship leaders have to provoke the people in hopes of creating a worship atmosphere so that when the man or woman of God walks in, the saints are programmed to respond!

Still, I enjoyed much of my fellowship with the ministry, and even though I wasn't a member, I began to tithe. I found the ministry trying to progress financially as many do these days in the areas of congregational growth. I didn't believe the ministry would take a wrong direction trying to meet goals, but I became suspicious when doctrine began infiltrating the atmosphere used in many prosperity messages! It takes a while before congregants begin to respond after constantly hearing about money, houses, cars, clothes, and other commodities, which are widely used when teaching about being prosperous!

Normally there are other authorities within the ministry which begin to co-sign/repeat what the pastor is preaching/teaching.

THE PRICE TAG

What I mean by this is; when pastors begins teaching on a particular subject, others in leadership, most times begin speaking the same things. Of course there should be unity and oneness within leadership, rather any kind of entity; but ministerial staffs are now pressured to speak and respond even when not in agreement. Therefore, you have idiots that come behind the authority trying to revamp what is being said, taking it to another level of possible foolishness. I found this to be the environment at GFT. I could hear the direction of where leadership wanted to go, but I knew there were obstacles preventing the ministry!

I couldn't seem to get past the major dilemma of leadership ministering to the people as if we were all women! There are certain ways you can minister to women and certain ways you can reach men, but when you're a ministry leader, you can't talk to your congregation as if they are all your girlfriends, even if it's predominantly women! I found myself lost many times, as the atmosphere began changing to the Gospel according to a woman and her purse, including the new or next husband now on the way!

I began visiting during the fall season, which was the wrong time, as many churches experience setbacks during the summer. I noticed some aggressive behavior regarding tithes and offering. I didn't want to begin making assumptions about the House, as I wasn't a member and felt many comments didn't pertain to me. So, I remained faithful and supported from within my capacity.

Pastor Hayes is the type of leader who knows her congregation. She would walk the sanctuary aisles and interact with congregants while delivering her messages. She comes across as a confident leader, while others could certainly say arrogant. She desires nothing less than the best for her local assembly, but her forward personality seemed to cause congregants to grow weary, kicking against the pricks! A few times during my fellowship, I've witnessed her openly revisiting congregant's personal testimonies. I'm not sure if individuals had testified privately or in public, but Pastor Hayes had outwardly re-language individual's past during a few of her sermons!

I found such behavior shocking and humiliating. I didn't need to hear the old sins of my brothers and sisters within the church. This was completely embarrassing demonstrating instantaneous humiliation! What would you think if you were a new member of the church, not really knowing anyone, and one Sunday the pastor pointed out a longtime member, outwardly saying that he or she was an ex-felon, former drug addict, or prostitute. I know we overcome by the Word of our testimonies, but I don't think it's wise to demonstrate this kind of revamping in an open forum. I guess congregants would have to be on edge! I'm sure it kept the saints/congregation from truly opening up and it probably caused damage to those with trust issues!

I guess when pastors find themselves in situations where congregants are not responding; some feel the need to try alternative methods obtaining what they want. Therefore, each week I began looking forward to the next episodic twist to an unfolding plot, as I began feeling leadership was up to something. As I mentioned earlier, the ministry was focused on congregational and financial growth, as members were pressured to bring others to church even participating in fund raising endeavors. This seems to always be the first steps when churches are executing a plan. As congregants extended visitation to others, of course the House must now structure itself to keep people coming! Many ministry leaders feel they now must execute many kinds of services, conventions and other type of events keeping individuals in attendance. Meanwhile, the primary focuses of these additional functions are fund raising ventures for the ministry.

THE PRICE TAG

It's now becoming common for congregants not to support many of the additional functions that ministries are executing, because we cannot afford them. They sound good as the announcer is reading the flyer, including the leader presiding service, trying to emphasize how powerful the event is going to be. But the reality that most congregants have now begun to pick up on is; how pressured they're going to feel affording the event! Now most times, the events are free; because when you place a ticket price, registration fee and/or admission, it seems to scare people away, so many have now structured events having no fees associated, but will use Seed Offerings and Money Lines to meet their budgets. Many leaders have found this to make them more money rather than wondering about listed prices! (Read Section 2.2)

Besides the constant turn to your neighbor every five minutes that began to drive me up the wall. I began to become annoyed by ministry associates pressuring me to join the church. Of course visitors could possibly equate to congregational growth, but new members could possible equate to more tithers! So week-by-week I've seemed to become a target, as I was already tithing, but I had not joined the ministry. If someone is doing the right thing, just leave him/her alone and allow the Spirit of God to direct him or her accordingly. But this ministry didn't seem to understand that, it was now time to harass someone because we need more men in the ministry anyway!

Every Sunday when it became time to open the doors of the church, leadership even members felt the need to leave their seats, walking around the sanctuary, trying to get non-members to join the church. I became furious with this behavior, which caused me to begin showing an unfriendly disposition to anyone that approached me thereafter. As soon as one person would walk away, the next person would jump up in my face running a repertoire about encouraging me to join the ministry. I instantly felt harassed, feeling I don't think this is the place for me.

The atmosphere of the ministry later grew intense as leadership began structuring services differently. As Wednesday nights were now being introduced as the time to begin your biblical introduction of how God wants His people to live prosperous. Midweek services were now structured teaching congregants the doctrine of prosperity. I knew what was happening before my eyes but became numb, not really feeling obligated because I wasn't a member of the ministry.

"Pastor Connect" better known as Wednesday night service, became frequently announced, as it was allegedly the direction to where God was calling the ministry. As the plot was clearly unfolding, I realized the approach obtaining the goals the ministry desired, was to use the prosperity doctrine. Many pastors have found this doctrine successful grooming their ministries, whereas now it's the notable strategy penetrating desiring assemblies! Not only does this doctrine encourages congregants, regarding God's desire for His people in the areas of finance and wealth, but when used incorrectly it causes suffering individuals, now feeling the need to pay for this alleged benefit from God!

The atmosphere at GFT began to aggressively change as leadership became demanding. Special offerings with increasing number of services; this was the typical symptom of knowing what the ministry was trying to accomplish. After feeling continually harassed to join the church, I knew this was not the place for me. After service one Sunday afternoon a male congregant of the church approached me a few blocks away, apologizing for actions used to solicit my membership over the past few weeks. That was the confirmation that I needed to release myself from this ministry!

THE PRICE TAG

I know you're wondering why I continue to connect myself with these kinds of ministries. It's almost like an individual who finds himself/herself always in personal relationships with the same type of people. It's not that I've sought these kinds of ministries but we must realize there are abrupt and massive changes now affecting many congregations around the world! Big business ideas to national recognition with other areas of notability are causing ministry leaders to restructure their assemblies—as was the case with the next ministry I was part of.

After departing Greater Faith Temple, I began fellowshipping with The Lord's Church Family Worship Center (TLC), where Bishop Eric A. McDaniel is pastor. I really enjoyed this ministry and felt at home because there were familiar faces I hadn't seen in many years. The atmosphere at TLC was progressive, as I'd come at a time when the church was outgrowing its current sanctuary. It appeared a new facility was the next move. I didn't attend every Sunday at first because I didn't want to find myself in a situation as when I fellowshipped at GFT. Although, this ministry didn't harass anyone to join, I wanted to maintain a sporadic fellowship.

During my fellowship at TLC, I began learning several aspects of the ministry, including its direction and progress over the years. I was very proud that the ministry had grown tremendously, as I was familiar with it foundation. I continued to inquire about the ministry because I begun to feel at home. In addition to the ministry pursuing a new facility, I discovered that the cathedral choir was preparing for its second live recording. I felt confident they would accomplish their goals. There wasn't any aggressive fundraising at the time, just basic rally Sundays, in which congregants formed teams to raise money for the new facility. Leadership advised the congregation of its desired budget, which was needed to close on the property (six-digit figure), whereas the rally teams would be diligent toward meeting the goal. There were also other endeavors put together helping the ministry get to this financial goal.

I didn't participate in any of the fundraising, as I was just a visitor and didn't want to get involved. I enjoyed the ministry of song and the preached Word and felt this was a good position for me at the time. During a Sunday morning service, there was an announcement that the ministry was no longer having services at the current location and would begin having them at the new location beginning Easter Sunday. I was amazed at how the ministry was progressing! Since I did not attend every Sunday, I wasn't able to understand how the church was pulling things together so quickly. I felt I should begin attending regularly, as I thought I was missing out on what was going on!

On April 11, 2004, (Easter Sunday), TLC resumed services at a new location, which was an old theatre. The first thing congregants began to realize is there was much work needed to be done to the building to make it appealing and operational! This Sunday would also be the first time that I was able to truly get some kind of idea of the size of the ministry. At the former location, there were two services on Sunday morning; now the theatre could hold everyone in one service. Of course, on Easter Sunday, hundreds of other congregants attend for their annual day for church, making it challenging to gauge the size of the ministry accurately.

The first month in the new location, leadership did indeed ask if we could consolidate services on Sunday, as this location could seat approximately fifteen to seventeen hundred individuals. I was shocked by the attendance; even with combined services, there was still more than enough room on the main level of the theatre, not even counting the two balconies! This puzzled me, as the ministry had the potential to pack the building!

I was so impressed with how the ministry had pulled things together, I inquired further about its future directions. I felt I should get behind it, supporting it during the transition. These feelings were developing as I continued to look around the theatre, noticing its condition. The tremendous amount of work that needed to be done would require money!

As we began settling into the new location during the first month, leadership began to stress the need for congregants to invite others to church because this building was obviously larger than the size of the ministry. Leadership continued to make mention of congregants being faithful with their tithes and offerings because the building needed improvements. During these announcements, it was mentioned that the church still hadn't closed on the building. Therefore, some fundraising endeavors were needed to reach the desired target for closure. I had begun to feel part of the ministry by this time; because I knew the scope of work that was needed, feeling I could contribute something, then being peaceful to begin returning tithes into this ministry.

I joined the ministry on April 18, 2004. I hadn't had a church home since West Angeles COGIC! I was happy with my decision and shared my personal transition with friends and family. This change bought about a different mind-set of how I approached ministry. I knew this commitment was serious, and I had to become dedicated to the leadership of the House. This wasn't my first church home, obviously, and I knew how to conduct myself and how to get behind a ministry. So when leadership continued to ask congregants to solicit others to attend the church for congregational growth purposes, that's what I did.

The first two months took some getting used to because in all transitions, there are always a few things that require more attention than others. But there seemed to be one thing that needed special attention and that was the offering! We were now falling under budget for our Sunday services, so leadership added an additional offering. After the preached Word, an additional offering then followed. At first it seemed this was a pressing need, so congregants began giving into the second offering. But the second offering didn't disappear. After the preached Word, someone would walk over to the Bishop with a number written on a little piece of paper, indicating that they needed more money!

Raising this second offering became a challenge after a while because congregants already knew they've given the first time. So in order to obtain this second offering on a regular basis, leadership communicated to the church the needs of the ministry. Congregants were told that we have to "step up on our giving." At this point, many congregants were probably thinking that meant they were closing on the property, but there were other calendar of events we were still hearing about as well.

Three months at the new facility had begun to reveal some things that began concerning me as a new member. I began to wonder why we were still hearing about closing on the property. During the time when I was just a visitor, even at the former location, I knew there were fundraising endeavors in place for this new facility, and now several months later, residing in the actual facility, why were we still fundraising to close on the property? Something at this point wasn't clear because I remembered hearing what the six-digit closing figure number was, and the ministry should have had that specific amount after numerous fundraising endeavors for over a four-month period or longer! Leadership continually began telling the congregation, "There is a possibility we could be closing on the theatre." We were almost there, so let's just get it done. Earnestly trying to help leadership reach its desired goal, congregants began giving above what they normally would.

THE PRICE TAG

For some reason, week after week, we were still hearing about being close to closing, but not really understanding the particulars of real estate or the operational structure of the ministry. Additional fundraising endeavors made their way to our attention. Proposed pledging plans, including a "Gideon's Army" seed-sowing group and other financial strategies were introduced! The atmosphere was changing to what I would have never thought could impact this church. Leadership became aggressive with congregants regarding returning the tithe; and of course tithing is the established principal for church, in which many congregants still choose not to do! So in order for the ministry to demonstrate or to make known who was and was not returning tithes, leadership created a weekly tithing list to be placed in the Sunday bulletin! This list was broken into categories, from leadership to choir members, etc., and showed readers the names of congregants who were returning tithes!

I was offended by this list and approached the head usher about whom I could speak to about having my name removed. Although you might be thinking that the list was no big deal, I began to believe the motive behind this listing was to embarrass those who were not returning the tithe! It was offensive to those who may struggle financially for whatever reason and it placed shame on them for not being obedient, meeting their obligation. My motive wasn't about me being a tither; it was about those who were not tithing, exempting them from embarrassment!

The head usher went to speak with one of the leaders, who approached me and asked why I had a problem with my name on the list. I explained my feelings about the ministry's motive behind the list and continued to stress that it was offensive and not wise! The ministry leader continued implying that the Bishop wanted to encourage those that weren't tithing by establishing the list.

That was the craziest thing I'd ever heard! There was no way the list was going to encourage people to do anything! If indeed this list obtains more names, it wasn't because individuals were encouraged; it was because individuals didn't want to be embarrassed! Of course there wasn't much I could do to have my name removed from the list, but I still felt the list was unwise. (Choir members and others, that served in the ministry, were restricted from their services, if found not returning tithes.)

It began to appear as if leadership had a weekly strategy for how to obtain more money because every Sunday there was something else. The disposition of Executive Pastor W. Brandon, who presided over Sunday morning service, would change right before offering. His practice was to come behind the message factor of the choir's last song, creating an atmosphere to sustain the worship, getting the people to another level of praise in time to receive offering.

It's a known fact among pastors, preachers, and other ministry leaders that you can easily obtain a good offering right after congregants are coming down from a certain level of praise and worship! (I openly rebuke the leader that will now try putting this into practice.) When congregants begin to dance, thereafter appeared to be the prime time to take up an offering! After a while, Pastor Brandon's practice became too rehearsed, and congregants would sit in their seats, looking at him as if he were crazy. This behavior escalated to him speaking in other tongues, to prophesying to the church, or those he knew something about (you know how that goes). Pastor Brandon's primary method for getting congregants to move according to his desire was to say, "I heard the Holy Spirit just say...." It was now the prime time to obtain what I believe, leadership needed to meet their financial goals! Congregants were then solicited to give specific amounts of money ranging from twenty to thirty dollars each! He would come right behind that statement, saying, "This has nothing to do with your regular Tithes and Offering." This was the pressure point for us to begin paying above our regular giving!

This portion of the service would take approximately fifteen to twenty minutes, as Pastor Brandon began to comb through the House for money, creating scenario after scenario to solicit people to move out of their seats to give; this became a typical strategy for receiving a "Seed Offering." Bishop McDaniel would sit quietly observe everything and he didn't stop his Executive Pastor.

Week after week, this was the environment we had to get used to. There was no way many of us could afford to give into an additional offering. If you couldn't afford to give the specific amounts being asked, you always have to wait until they finally get down to your specified dollar amount; which about time they would get down to possibly five dollars, it would then be stated: "Just come with whatever you have; everybody should be bringing something!" This is now the atmosphere of thousands of churches, structuring the House for specific amounts of money! Isn't it a shame that our leaders are now telling us how much money they want? How dare leadership tell congregants a specified amount of money to bring as offering! That's like asking the woman in the Bible who had given a penny, if she needed any change!

Even with the additional offering, we still hadn't closed on the building. Every week there was a continual announcement about us being close to closing on the property, and how the cathedral choir was still preparing for its second live recording! How were we still affording ministry luxuries while renting two facilities and trying to close on one? I began piecing things together.

These changes ushered a different atmosphere into the ministry. I knew for sure that when congregants got home, there was plenty to discuss on the phone regarding the latest episodic endeavors of the ministry. We were becoming adapted to a manipulative environment, not really believing what was happening before our eyes. You would have never believed Bishop to be associated with any of this behavior, because his meek and gentle reputation belied the changes. We were all shocked!

This hostile environment caused congregants to withdraw their attendance on a weekly basis! And looking around the sanctuary, you could see that others chose not to attend church regularly. Congregants were even vanishing from midweek services and then being harassed on Sundays for not attending! In addition, congregants were arriving late on Sunday mornings, trying to avoid Pastor Brandon's deceptive weekly performance. But that didn't change anything because leadership had already figured out that congregants were rebelling. By received offering after the Word, this became the final opportunity to get from the people!

Why should congregants even find themselves in situations, where they're purposely rebelling from leadership? Why should we find ourselves more depressed leaving the building than when we arrived? It's almost as if we're trying to protect ourselves from abuse! So we purposely do the opposite of what is begin asked because we already know that doing what leadership is telling us is the right thing is going to cause us pain! This kind of behavior causes congregants to sin, because we're trying to protect our feelings and emotions, while still being supportive. Well, I must admit that I began to rebel as well! As the summer season approached, I already knew what was coming. I knew for sure it wasn't going to be time for a weekly praise meeting, but for a weekly abusive beating! If we were beat up during the spring, imagine the summer season.

A celebrity pastor from Long Island, New York, visited our church (pre-New York call Service August 2005); and Bishop

McDaniel, the choir, musicians, and even the congregation showed off at our pleasure. I realized that night on my way home that pastors showcase their choirs and churches; I suppose to flex a muscle while demonstrating the ability/capacity of the House. Bishop most likely had his personal reasons, for that night he was polished and ready to shine! Sometimes you never know what goes on between pastors and other ministry leaders, but those stories would fly off a bookshelf.

Our regular services are challenged on occasion, but I guess when there are invited guest(s) in the House, most folks pull out the good silverware and dishes for serving! We all were jokingly threatened to demonstrate a façade of a progressive ministry that evening, but if folks knew the truth, they would have chosen another location to conduct the event! There has always been a stigma about churches in The Bronx; therefore, for many years congregants in Brooklyn and other boroughs wouldn't attend our services. The Bronx sets the trend for what many have desired to accomplish for years, if it wasn't for The Bronx... (Enough Said).

All the hard-working individuals that support pastors in the spotlight are typically never appreciated, but are expected to join into the pride game! What a horrible demonstration before the saints, as we're already messed up, believing God loves us more than un-repented sinners! These demonstrations divide us from reaching an un-repented sinner, including speaking to other believers! We as believers are even divided among each other, not even speaking to a fellow congregant that we know by face. We could be on the bus together on the way to the same church and we can't even say, "Praise the Lord" to a fellow congregant. What has happened to us, or rather what is happening to us? (We must begin investigating our authorities.)

As usual, many churches experience decrease in congregational attendance in the summer, and for the entire month of July, I didn't attend church. I stayed home, upset that I was a member of the kind of ministry I'd tried to stay away from. I became so angry that I didn't have anything good to say about the ministry. Friends questioned how my feelings could take such a drastic turn so abruptly, but I couldn't seem to convey peaceful feelings. When individuals are abused by people they love, it becomes difficult to convey real emotions because the abuse leaves the individual confused, believing it's their fault!

Many ministry leaders will tell you how the ministry is good ground, as if their ministry is the only place where believers should sow. But what about the lives of believers? Why is it we have to always support the man or woman of God, holding their arms up, interceding while supporting all of their desires, meanwhile exhausting (ripping and running) our lives until we're poor and unable to even help ourselves? Then when we're unable to support from a decreasing self-capacity, then we're called rebellious and even backsliders! How is it that the House is the only good ground? Guess what? Believers are good soil, not the administrative structures of the House! We're the Body of Christ; the Spirit of Christ Jesus lives and works through the lives of believers! So why isn't there any sowing into us? We're the ones that will produce a harvest as God gives the increase! Right now I need you to do me a quick favor. I want you to look into a mirror and say out loud, "I am good ground!" Then say it again!

For so long, we've been taught incorrectly that the House is the only place to plant/sow, but realistically it's only an administrative forum, established to operate/gathering those that are called to serve! Have you ever had a revelation of yourself (a look at potentials that rest, rule and abide in your life inspired by the Holy Spirit)?

That's right, you have the same Holy Ghost and it shouldn't be overlooked, but operating in concordance, orderly and peaceful! There are aspects of our lives as believers that require us to sow into our own dreams. That's because there are things the Holy Spirit will show us, purposed for our own destiny; which requires sowing into what God has given and/or showing us! But now our leaders are teaching us that if we're not sowing into the House, whatever else we're pursuing isn't relevant or of God! They're severally quoting that *Our destiny is tied into the man or woman of God we're under* utilizing this scenario now controlling people!

I can't tell you how many times I've had to hear a man or woman of God actually tell congregants, *If you make things happen for me, things will begin happening for you.* But the truth is that our lives begin lacking as we support everything that our leaders speak as the next move of God! How can we keep up with all the things they're telling us *God is calling us to do?*

So again I ask, what about the lives of believers? When do we get to focus or meditate on what the Spirit is showing us? Do you believe the Holy Spirit even requires us to meditate on the direction of own lives? We're not all called to preach, sing, and occupy the four walls of the House. There are thousands of things the Holy Spirit is willing to show us, having an impact in the world by allowing Him to first reveal our own destiny; then allowing the revelation to further open our hearts to the teaching/leading of the Holy Spirit.

Pastors and ministry leaders will always tell you how the Spirit of God fills their temples, and everything else to self-promote the name of the House. You should realize it's the same strategy as marketing and promotions. Many pastors have structured their churches aggressively just to keep up with the latest trends of other ministries! Trying to keep up with other ministries can place yours in bankruptcy, meanwhile, burdening and stressing your congregants. You can't believe the hype; the proof is definitely in the pews!

I returned to church on the last Sunday of July, and the entire month was to be "Church without Walls," as the congregation was going to have services outdoors. This particular Sunday, changes were made and services were now resumed in the theatre. Feeling remorseful, I needed reconciliation regarding my thoughts of the ministry. I was angrier with myself for not allowing more time to possibly fellowship with the church before joining. Many thoughts filled my mind, as this was the second time I'd contemplated leaving. By this time I was only a member for a little over ninety days! How could a church environment drastically change in a short period of time? This definitely was not the environment at the former location; and if so, maybe those were the weeks during my sporadic fellowship.

I sat very quietly during this reconciliation period because I needed to understand why I was drawn to the ministry and desiring to leave at the same time. I desired to leave a month or so earlier but changed my mind after gaining understanding of how some pastors work so hard for years, and sometimes situations don't necessarily turn around until later! I could totally identity and understand this, as it was the cycle of my life as well! Bishop McDaniel deserves everything his heart desires and those were my prayers for him as a member. But I personally believe he had the wrong type of people around him! There is a huge quality difference between his family and those that serve under him. I don't observe the same characteristics from other leadership officials within the ministry, as with Bishop Eric McDaniel and Co-Pastor Subrenia McDaniel!

THE PRICE TAG

It was now ordination time at The Lord's Church Family Worship Center, as this was the time to learn more about the ministry regarding other pastors and ministers being ordained, and those previously ordained that now pastor their own churches. It was interesting looking around the sanctuary and observing clergy in uniformed attire. This was one of the most orderly services I'd experienced at the church, as the House had a little problem with setting order! As services proceeded as scheduled, many noticed that Bishop was not in attendance. Many thought possibly he was running a little late. Co-Pastor Subrenia McDaniel was finally in service on time; she was known to arrive late, making a first lady entrance after service had already started.

The atmosphere grew wary because the Bishop wasn't there at the ordination service. As congregants began growing restless, wondering where he was, Co-Pastor Subrenia McDaniel had to take the platform to sooth the House. She explained that the Bishop had to accept an outside preaching engagement, in hopes of further supporting the ministry during a crucial period for the church. But she was being evasive and congregants picked up on it. But we rarely hear her talk, so the congregation was just happy to hear her voice. She continued to explain, how grateful she was to have Bishop Jody Brady of The River Church in Raleigh, North Carolina, be with us to conduct the ordination service in the Bishop's absence.

We all knew what we heard, but it didn't make any sense at all! Why would the Bishop of our assembly choose to accept an outside preaching engagement not in attendance to ordain his own clergy? We all knew it was Bishop's earnest desire to obtain a mortgage on the theatre and we all tried as much as we'd could to support him during prior months. So this incident seemed to be an extreme decision!

That wasn't the entire story, as Bishop Brady was the mouthpiece to spill the real deal! After the preached Word, Bishop Brady told the congregation that during the next part of the service, he was going to become carnal with the people. That didn't shock us, as he had definitely proven carnal many times during his message. He explained that we were about to lose the theatre. He further explained that the mortgage company wanted the rest of the money by Monday (the next day). Needless to say, we were not prepared for such a shock.

We all knew we'd been working hard for months to support the vision and didn't understand why we hadn't been able to close on the property. I knew this couldn't have been the easiest thing for Bishop Brady to tell the people since he wasn't our pastor. Why couldn't our own pastor face his congregation and just tell us what was really going on with the ministry. Bishop Brady continued to explain that the mortgage company desired twenty-seven thousand additional dollars before closure. Where were we going to get that kind of money in less than twenty-four hours? Bishop Brady told the congregation he wasn't leaving until he had raised all the money!

Congregant's ears, eyes, mouths, wallets, and purses began to pop open as he begun to comb the ministry for money! He stated he was going to give either seven or nine thousand dollars to start the process and that the House could contribute the rest. He began his "Money Line" with one thousand dollars and proceeded to work the House until he was sure he had the rest of the money. He had to use every scenario he could think of to get congregants to give!

Congregants were solicited to give rent and mortgage money from our homes, advised to max out our credit cards, empty our checking and savings accounts, borrow money from friends and family, or however we could get money in order to support the ministry! He explained that it was the same practice done within his assembly. He later justified these remarks by telling us that it's better for us to have a place to praise God! I guess when your congregation winds up homeless due to eviction or foreclosure, it's better to have a place to praise God, but the truth is there's very little to no refuge for those that attend church!

Bishop Brady was very serious about raising the money, and I believe he was sent PURPOSELY to take care of the job! It is known that pastors solicit the help of those who allegedly possess a gift for raising money. Bishop McDaniel had been trying to solicit the people to give more with the depressing help of his Executive Pastor. But people had grown weary with the tactics used and decided not to comply. Therefore, it was allegedly necessary to import the help of someone else to prostitute the ministry for twenty-seven thousand dollars in less than twenty-four hours!

Bishop Brady knew what he was doing and there was no shame in his game! Sometimes when pastors begin conducting seed offerings there is a kickback of funds distributed to their own pockets as well. The only thing I appreciate about his tactic was that he honestly told us before executing his plot that he was going to be carnal with the people. He even purposely missed his flight back to Raleigh, North Carolina, that late afternoon, not leaving until he'd combed the House for every cent he could get!

This plot took over ninety minutes as congregants grew tired and hungry after being in service for over four hours. During this prostitution sting, congregants were made aware that Bishop Brady has raised hundred of thousands for his own church, and after obtaining his desired budget, advised the congregation that the Holy Spirit allegedly told him to preach for several weeks a message called (paraphrased) "Get Out!" This message was to encourage congregants to leave the ministry! How can you raise all that money from those supporting your ministry on a weekly basis and then ask them to leave after getting what he wanted? You preach us happy, take our money, and then kick us in the aspirin on our way out the door, continuing this cycle every week!

Money lines are known to take a lot of time and are targeted to help ministry leaders obtain specific amounts of money. We were all in service so long that Bishop Brady became so hungry that one of the associates of TLC went to McDonald's and purchased a Quarter Pounder with cheese combo, as if that were going to satisfy his hanging belly. He stood right on the pulpit eating his hamburger and still combing the House for money! This was indeed my signal to get to stepping; at that point, I had enough. I handed my last five dollars in my wallet to the usher and proceeded to leave the sanctuary.

Outside the theatre were angry congregants not knowing what to say, needing someone to talk to, allowing time to release frustration ambushed upon their hearts. It was bad enough the ministry wasn't in a desirable area of The Bronx, including members were not annually grossing fifty to sixty thousand dollars (speculating). How can people just rob from the poor and feel as if it's God's will to prosper? God's people are so delicate, as many have experienced similar situation when involved in "Old Sin Nature" and now experiencing reflective behavior in church. These kinds of things make it very difficult for believers to reach those who have been hurt by the church.

The following Sunday would be the anticipated time to hear from Bishop McDaniel. Maybe he addressed the situation during midweek service, but when Sunday morning arrived, he didn't say a word! By this time, we were confident that the ministry had finally reached it target and have fulfilled its demand with the mortgage company. Executive Pastor W. Brandon advised the congregation

THE PRICE TAG

that TLC would be going back to the former location in a few weeks, as they would be conducting renovation at the theatre! He further explained that the next time we returned to the theatre, we wouldn't even recognize it. Continuing to detail the forecasted remodeling that would take place in the theatre; this would be a reason to go back to the former location.

I guess this was news to advise the congregation that we had finally closed on the theatre, although it was never said directly. All the aggressive fundraising was most likely now over, but as I looked around the sanctuary, it was evident that the events of several weeks had clearly turned people away from the ministry. I was so annoyed by this outcome that I sent an email to the church expressing my feelings. I implied in the email that there is corruption in the church's leadership, as it was driving congregants away, knowing that we need as many as we can, to afford the theatre! I continued to state how I would sit and pray, waiting for Bishop McDaniel to set order in the House!

For a few weeks I continued to be faithful, as new changes were now being implemented into the ministry. During regular services it was a custom to receive tithes and offerings before the preached Word; now it was scheduled after! This strategy was implemented now having congregants participating in a seed offering on a weekly basis! Leadership had figured out that they could get more money by structuring a seed offering vs. having freewill offering. These changes had structured the ministry, as if we were now paying for the Word!

As these changes began to become trend, congregants began to set their personal trends as well. Therefore, right after the preached Word, congregants would then begin to make their way out the door before the seed offering solicitation would begin. This would make it very difficult to conduct altar call since there would now appear walking up the aisles, imposed to individuals walking down the aisles! You can't blame congregants and start fussing with them about being out of order. There is a reason why many choose to be disobedient, trying to protect themselves in other areas! Why were we still conducting aggressive fundraising, as it seemed we have finally closed on the property? This puzzled me as I became suspicious, regarding now we needed to come up renovation budgeting. Well, if the ministry struggled to raise the six-digit figure needed for closing, imagine, raising money to renovate an old theatre; it would cost over a million dollars! Why does leadership think congregants have no clue how things work? By this time, my mind was completely numb, just going through the motions of giving what I could and going home complaining!

I must continue to stress that the ministry was still affording luxuries during the entire process as the cathedral choir was still preparing for its second live recording! From my experiences in media and entertainment, I knew that a live recording over the course of two nights at a performing arts theatre could cost up to nearly fifty thousands dollars! Where were we going to get that money? Was there a record label behind this venture, or would the ministry be footing the bill? Putting the pieces together didn't take much time, and I figured out what had been going on with the ministry's money!

As the live recording was approaching, it was now time for leadership to place demands on us to purchase tickets. Congregants were solicited to purchase two tickets to attend the events held over two nights. A table was set up in the atrium of the theatre to stop congregants on their way out of the building to further obligate them to attend. Bishop McDaniel was serious about the congregation attending the recording stating; "If TLC were the only ones in attendance, there should be a decent number of people there."

THE PRICE TAG

I purposely wasn't trying to afford any further endeavors of the ministry other than returning my tithes and giving offering; therefore, I wasn't planning to attend.

Bishop McDaniel continued to accept outside preaching engagements as Co-Pastor McDaniel was scheduled to deliver the Word on the last Sunday in September in the theatre. Although much had transpired during the summer and into the fall, she testified about much of her tests as well! It was good to hear another voice, as she is in-fact leadership in the ministry; congregants were open to receive her. But the congregation at this time was experiencing lack in attendance; therefore, she initiated the seed offering conception as well!

Arriving church on that Sunday Morning, we noticed ushers conducting individuals to the center section of the theatre. Everyone immediately noticed that a portion of the roof of the building had collapsed so the left area of the auditorium was closed. This appeared to be a major problem as it was evident the building needed renovation. To our surprise that was the last Sunday we had services in the theatre, as we were told to return back to the former location beginning the next Sunday. Would renovations begin soon? Was the building insured, whereas if there were any further situations, there would be no insurance claims in the works? Or now that the live recording was just one week away, it was now time to head back to the former location, regarding the ministry having the money needed?

Returning back to the prior location seemed a little strange because we've spent six months away and were returning to a smaller place. Over the course of several months the ministry had grown; therefore, I was sure the building wouldn't have the capacity, now inconveniencing congregants. Although midweek services were still held at this location while we were occupying the theatre, I'd seemed to have forgotten the building's overall capacity. When I arrived I thought to myself, why did we leave here in the first place? If the sanctuary had just undergone some improvements, we could have stayed here, possibly just adding an additional service to accommodate overflow. I guess three services on Sunday morning would appear too much, but many ministries have several services before inquiring a new facility.

This particular Sunday we had a guest preacher since Bishop McDaniel was on vocal rest for the cathedral choir was having a continuation of their live recording during that evening. (I'm choosing to leave out the name of the visiting preacher; his fellowship with the ministry was new and he walked into something he probably wasn't prepared for.) I remember services starting nearly an hour late, as the earlier service overlapped into the other. As service began, it was sure a High Time in the sanctuary, as a praiseful atmosphere filled the building. I guess being back at this location was a relief!

After the preached Word, tithes and offerings was the next order of business, as the visiting preacher asked the Bishop, about taking up an offering. Many preachers ask if there is a specific need in the House, which in turn encourages the man or woman of God who delivered the Word to then proceed with the offering. Of course TLC would have a need; therefore, the visiting preacher began to seed offering the people for thirty dollars each. As mentioned earlier, many times when a preacher chooses to conduct a seed offering there is a kickback of funds given to the preacher as well. The new structure still confused congregants, as it was typical for leadership to further explain how the requested amount of money had nothing to do with congregant's regular tithes and offerings. This practice still solicited congregants to pay above what they would normally give, to situate the House having one offering, requesting specific amounts of money, in addition to congregant's tithes and offerings.

On the following week, I received an email response in reply to the email that I initially sent to the church. The church's secretary replied stating; Executive Pastor W. Brandon wanted to meet with me on the coming Sunday and requested that I call the church office to arrange the meeting. I was shocked that I would receive a reply email from the church because my message had been rather straightforward. Personally believing that Pastor Brandon was a primary suspect for corruption in the leadership, I replied back to the email, stating, "I decline to meet with Pastor Brandon, as I will continue to sit and pray." I wasn't a congregant in whom leadership would have known my name; I was just a member who would attend church and then would leave, limiting my fellowship.

When church service had ended on that Sunday, I made my way to the exit. A minister blocked me at the door, asking if I was Brother Johnson. He stated that Pastor Brandon would like to speak to me, and I told him that in my email reply, I'd declined to meet with him. He stated that I should follow him! You would think I was under arrest, as I was blocked at an exit door of the church. He proceeded to walk back into the sanctuary as I stood there, still wondering why someone would block me from leaving. He turned and noticed that I was not following, stating again, that I should come with him, as he was determined to execute his order!

As we approached the front of the church, Pastor Brandon was speaking with someone as I was advised to have a seat until he was finished. Before he was finished speaking to a fellow congregant, he interrupted by advising me that he would be with me shortly. I sat puzzled about how they knew who I was. I didn't send my email from a blind email address, so the recipient wouldn't be able to know whom it's from. I had stated my name as a member and detailed my true feelings regarding the ministry.

As I was waiting for Pastor Brandon to wrap up his conversation, this was the time to take a deep breath, as I knew I had to bind up my flesh in order to now approach leadership of the ministry. I was escorted to a little room stage left of the pulpit, and Pastor Brandon made sure to clear the room for us to talk privately. He introduced himself, as I was lead to limit what I would say; regarding my email had already deliberated my feelings. He started the conversation by asking, "Is there a problem?" What? You would think he would open with a quick word of prayer or something that would signify some kind of leadership and congregant connection, but I was asked, is there a problem? He wouldn't have been able to understand my answer to that question if I chose to answer it. So I replied, "I didn't request to see you; you requested to see me."

He asked if I could speak up and then stated that he'd received my email and was apologetic regarding not getting back to me sooner. This was due to the ministry transitioning back to the former location and the cathedral choir's live recording. I interrupted by asking how did he know it was me. He replied, "It's my job; it took me about two to three days to figure it out, but I knew who you were." That response didn't sound logical since there are only about four people in the entire ministry who knew me by name. His response clearly startled me, as I didn't know it was now the obligation of leadership to know everyone by name and face! I asked him if he found my email offensive. *How did my simple email get me here in this room?* When members join the church, the ministry assigns each new member a caretaker; a member's first point of contact if indeed a situation arises. So I asked why my caretaker hadn't called or approached me regarding my email.

THE PRICE TAG

Why would the Executive Pastor have his alleged assistant block me at the church's exit doors, desiring to speak with me?

Pastor Brandon began thanking me for being faithful, as he explained it's his job to respond to emails and the administrative concerns of the ministry. Thanking me for being faithful puzzled me as well, and I asked him if he checked to see if I was a tither before approaching me, and his answer was still, "It's my job!" From this point on, I knew what kind of situation I was involved in!

Pastor Brandon began asking me some questions about my background, trying to feel me out and see if we knew the same folks, I guess. He asked what church I'm formerly been a member of, as it was evident I wasn't a new convert sending an email detailing seasoned language regarding corruption in leadership! I advised him I was a former member of West Angeles COGIC. He continued to tell me a little about his background and position in the ministry as I quietly wondered when he was going to get to the point!

Our conversation didn't come across as he thought it would. Maybe he thought I was going to act ghetto, yelling and screaming about specific details of the ministry. I don't think he was prepared for my disposition as we found ourselves winging the conversation. I remember him asking me how long I was a member of the church, and I really became suspicious after him telling me twice that it was his job to know these things! If that's the case, he would know the members, and that I'd joined six months ago! I would think my membership materials would reflect this information. If he took the time to check and see if I was returning my tithes, why didn't he take the time to locate my member information as well? I guess when you have a faithful tither making a complaint, there is a certain way to approach the individual, because ministries are already prepared to approach those whom are not returning tithes or supporting the ministry!

This didn't seem as an interrogation, but I was still puzzled how my email got me in the presence of the person I believe allegedly responsible for some corruption. I again asked him what he thought about my email. He stated, "There is corruption in all ministries!" Oh, really! Well, this was news to me. He continued to explain that as the Executive Pastor of TLC, he tries to handle situations such as mine without getting Bishop McDaniel involved. He felt that Bishop McDaniel should be focused on preaching and other aspects of the ministry! Well, I don't believe Bishop McDaniel to be naive to the things of the House, as he's always thinking and watching, and not quick to say much. So I didn't believe that the Bishop didn't know about my email. If indeed he truly didn't know, I'm sure the word would have been out soon enough!

As our conversation was clearly running out of words, I stressed to Pastor Brandon that I didn't want the privacy of this meeting to interrupt my worship as a member of the ministry. He assured me that it wouldn't, jokingly stating that the next time he saw me, he'd just say, "Praise the Lord, Brother Johnson," and that's it! I continued by asking who was the person that blocked me at the door, because clearly he wasn't the church secretary that replied to my email. He stated that the individual was his assistant, who helps him with many administrative aspects of the church.

We ended our conversation by shaking hands as I proceeded to leave the room. I couldn't wait to get out of the building, as I immediately felt disturbed by the meeting. This experience made several thoughts flood my mind asking myself how my email—out of all the emails, letters, and phone calls this church could possibly receive—get me in the presence of the Executive Pastor. In addition, thinking that I could have possibly done something wrong, or had made a very bold accusation that could have been incorrect!

THE PRICE TAG

That evening I made several calls to other believers that I know who had read the actual email that I sent the church. Two individuals had read the email before I sent it, making sure I wasn't saying anything offensive, not speaking out of anger or the leading of another spirit! Their feelings were just as mine, that my email was on eye opener, clearly advising leadership that someone was watching and was serious about what was transpiring in the ministry. This encouraged me to continue taking a stand, because there is surely hundreds in the ministry that desire to do what I have done but are fearful!

Several individuals that I conversed with regarding the email, including the meeting that followed, stated, Pastor Brandon was probably guilty, whereas he earnestly had to shake down the ministry to find out who I was! He did ask me in the room if the Holy Spirit showed me something about the ministry. This was probably to inquire about a specific office in the Body of Christ; maybe he thought I was a prophet bringing warning to the House. (Who really knows?)

I discovered a few days later that some of Pastor Brandon's remarks were not true, as I called a fellow member and asked if someone approached her regarding me. She stated that Pastor Brandon had my name on a little piece of paper, asking everybody do you know this person; she said it went on for a few weeks. When he finally asked her, she pointed me out during service. After speaking with her about what had transpired from that incident, she became very annoyed that she had become involved in something she knew nothing about. She became inquisitive regarding what was going on, as I didn't share any information. I didn't want her worship to be affected by present situations within the ministry.

On the approaching Sunday it seemed strange that I would continue to attend a ministry that I believed was corrupt by leadership. I didn't want my personal feelings to get in the way of my primary reason for attending church, and I really had to focus during service in order to block out personal feelings. I seemed to be able to see past the prior weeks, being able to enter into the presence of God as if nothing had happened, but I noticed some individuals in the congregation had begun looking at me strange!

Because I was a member that no one really knew, I thought it strange that I would now see fellow congregants smiling and nodding at me and wanting to shake my hand! During offering time, a fellow congregant I didn't know walked by and touched me on my shoulder as he returned to his seat. Information had certainly leaked into the congregation. (We all know how the saints like to talk.)

To my surprise, on my way home that Sunday I was led to peacefully leave the ministry. I was only a member from Sunday April 8, until Sunday October 17, of 2004, exactly six months. I couldn't understand how this entire experience made six months seem like two years! What was I going to do now? Where was I going to worship next? Taking such a bold stand to protect my heart, and possibly the hearts of others, had caused me to view ministry with different eyes. Could I have just swept my feelings under the rug and continued to attend, while supporting as if nothing had happened or was going on? Is that what millions of congregants are doing these days? Could I have just enjoyed the church services, continuing to go home depressed, complaining about the latest episodic endeavors of the ministry? Or do you just sit and become numb as if you're crazy, being abused meanwhile being told that the House is best for you! (I don't think so.)

For several days I placed blame on myself, believing that God had sent me to a ministry, and then I allowed the enemy to use inconsistencies within myself possibly to cause interruption! These thoughts allowed me to look back at all the ministries that I've been apart of to really understand that possibly I am the one with the problem! Meditating on these thoughts, I started to become angry with myself for allowing so much time to go by before realizing that I was possibly moving in the wrong direction!

During this period of my life, I was in pre-production for a syndicated radio show in which I recorded a segment called: "Who Do You Call When the Pastor Is out of Control?" The segment had received so much attention, whereas listeners immediately identified with the message. It was becoming clear that the message held great relevancy, as people wanted to understand further how several abrupt changes were now affecting hundreds, possibly thousands of assemblies!

I approached *Gospel Today* magazine to publishing an article regarding this subject matter. I received a response back from the magazine, which required me to obtain the objective truth to the subject. The objective truth was to hear the other side of the story! I began putting the article together and found this subject matter to increase before my eyes. I discovered that during my journalistic efforts to document several aspects of church and what we call sanctuary worship services, the article was becoming too long! There was no way a magazine would publish over ten pages of relevant information, not including the objective truth that was required! I realized that the subject was greater than could be contained in an article, greater than just a radio segment, but should be an in-hand tool in which congregants can obtain information regarding several aspects of ministry.

This experience has forever changed my life, as I no longer am placing blame on myself. As of today, TLC, my former church that I loved, has not closed on the theatre! I called the theatre owners directly on two occasions and have verified this information for myself. I also called a fellow member of the church and was advised that the ministry still hasn't taken the honest initiative to tell the people that all of their hard work and financial support were used for something other than what they believed! I've also have become aware that the ministry has decreased in size, as now caretakers are calling members, soliciting them to attend services. Congregants must have been asking about the theatre, for the ministry stated in the church bulletin that if congregants had any concerns about the theatre to send an email to the church!

I wonder how long it's going to take the ministry to tell the people there is no more theatre. I wonder if they even care that they have deceived the people to believe in a vision that probably wasn't real! Even if executed endeavors didn't work out as planned, congregants can truly understand, as we try personal endeavors ourselves that sometimes don't workout. But I personally believe leadership has a responsibility to demonstrate honesty regarding fundraising endeavors they implement!

As of today, I have no hard feelings regarding what I'd given into the ministry, for what was given, was from my heart and not from my flesh, guilt or for transaction! Therefore, I can peacefully move on, knowing that whatever harvest is due me, I will receive in some other way. But I am confident and determined to make sure ministries will no longer be able to manipulate their congregants, sending them away angry, confused, doubting, and even wavering in their faith—believing God to be associated with these dealings! This has been the seed for *The Price Tag*.

Again, I do apologize to any pastor or ministry leader that was mentioned in this chapter or elsewhere in this book as a way of relevancy for my voice! It is not my intention to destroy your ministry, or to have others make decisions not supporting your ministry. But this message is one that is bold, strong, and aggressive, certain to cause several kinds of changes around the world! If you personally feel I have caused damage to your business entity or ministry, you are open and free to send me an invitation to see a judge, as my contact information is listed in this publication. Until then, I will continue to market this publication around the world in various languages and to fund, while setting forth every precautionary measure listed in this publication!

Congregants around the world need to be aware that our sanctuaries are in serious trouble! Therefore, this publication is just the beginning, as I'm confident restoration is coming for congregants who have been abused and mistreated, wondering with nowhere to go!

Who would have thought the day would ever come when congregants would begin waking up, realizing their lives as good soil? As each day progresses, I'm looking forward to seeing my brothers and sister reflecting nothing less than the purchased possession that lives within us already! We don't have to buy, lease, or finance it because it's already given: the Holy Ghost empowers us completely. Amen!

CHAPTER TWO

IT'S OFFERING TIME IN THE SANCTUARY
(Applause)

2.1 Concerning Our Tithes and Offering

Why do we give offering? I know you're thinking this is a ridiculous question! But you'll be surprised how many congregants don't possess knowledge about why we bring offering into the House. Many believe the reason for bringing offering is to help the poor, while others feel good just giving to charity. Many believe offering is to support pastors or other ministry leaders, while others feel it's to help the ministry for operation costs. There are possibly numerous reasons why congregants decide to give offering, but many are not aware that there is a historical/spiritual history about its foundation.

Many ministry leaders frequently visit the subject of tithing, but rarely give much teaching in regards to offering. We're just told to "Bring an Offering" (Leviticus 1:2, 27:9, I Chronicles 16:29,

Psalms 96:8, 66:20), but these Scriptures don't give us any historic understanding for why congregants for centuries have been giving offering. You'll discover throughout the Old Testament of the Bible that God the Father himself established offering! You will find in (Genesis 4) that Cain brought unto the Lord the fruit of the ground as an offering. Was agricultural harvest the only kind of offering in the Bible days? No. You'll find in the same chapter that Abel brought of the firstlings of his flock and of their fat portions.

Throughout our biblical history both men and women came, all willing hearted as they brought to the Lord their offerings: freewill, votive, sacrificial offerings, drink, flock, burnt offerings, gold, silver, bronze, jewelry, and gold objects of every kind. Today we have legal tender (money). Tithing, vows, and sacrificial offerings differ from freewill offering, as the latter is freedom of choice in what is brought to God. So why are our pastors and ministry leaders requesting specific amounts of money? God is pleased when we bring offering and there are times when he's not pleased with our offering (read Section 2.4).

In (Exodus 25:2, I Chronicles 29:6-7), we read that the tabernacle needed to be built, and later re-built (Ezra 2:68-69); therefore God commanded an offering to be received. The people decided by their own freewill, as to how much they were going to give. There was no stipulation as to how much each should give and there was no reward or penalty for those that had given larger and/or smaller amounts. Freewill offering isn't measured by an actual amount; it's given from what the individual can afford! The nation was to provide the resources, but only those who were willing to give to the work were to contribute. God had already called those he'd chosen, but there was a requirement for a willing supply of materials to carry out the tasks (Exodus 35:29-34). This is an example of a type of "Freewill Offering;" God sets the target and we regard whether we can reach it! When God sets to have a specific work completed, the people of God are to join together; collectively contributing whatever their hearts will lead them to give. Without God's people (the Body of Christ) coming together as one, the work of the Kingdom could experience setbacks!

Does this mean that whatever our ministry leaders desire as a target for the House is what we must aim for? No, definitely not! The target is what God sets for the House; it's what He desires to be done! The target will certainly come by way of revelation of God and be confirmed by His wisdom, but it's not the responsibility of our leaders to begin choosing targets: soliciting congregants to give specific amounts of money for freewill offering, including praying segregated prayers for those that give larger amounts, and biased prayers for those who can only give from a limited capacity!

The responsibility of our pastors and ministry leaders is to seek God's direction for the House, followed by discussions with other leadership officials. Many ministries don't involve congregants in any decision-making endeavors of the church, as many no longer have scheduled church meetings discussing the latest endeavors of the ministry. Congregants are no longer aware of how their contributions are being implemented into the ministry, nor are we aware of the ministry's strategy for operation! Many times, we're just ambushed with calendars of events, which we're then told and sometimes pressured to govern ourselves accordingly! This practice is increasingly becoming tiresome, as congregants cannot keep up with all the events our ministries are now pressing! It is the continual obligation of leadership to strengthen the organizational structures of the House, but now congregants are beginning to become so overwhelmed; we're not even sure if many of the scheduled targets are from God or another initiation of fundraising not revealed to the people!

THE PRICE TAG

Basic necessities of the House are not specific targets initiated by our leaders, then implementing fundraising committees funding endeavors! We must bring an offering so our churches and ministries can acquire their necessities for operation. Many congregants don't understand that it costs money to operate a ministry. I know you've heard of ministry leaders making mention of this repeatedly, because it does cost money to keep a ministry in operation. Just as it requires money to keep a roof over your head, maintain bills to keep your utilities current, and purchase other necessities to operate your household, a church requires the same things and sometimes more.

Congregants for too many years have been taking advantage of church! We come when we feel like it; we disrespect the House by not returning the tithe. Many don't think that it costs money to keep toilet tissue in the bathrooms, as well as provide paper towels, drinking cups, water fountains, soap, offering envelopes, programs, and many other necessities in order to operate a ministry! Many churches have committees established for feeding and clothing the unfortunate, as well as other types of outreach supports that require financial backing!

On the flip side, it's becoming common for ministries to thrust themselves into higher financial brackets, and then soliciting their congregants to give more to support them! For example, if your ministry leader purchases a new home, then begins to solicit congregants to step up on their giving in order to afford the new luxury, this is not proper protocol for operating a ministry. Pastors and leaders can absolutely stress their congregations by trying to afford aggressive luxuries!

Congregants are to bring an offering unto the Lord, being symbolic of our expressions of love and support for Kingdom building. We don't give offering to support our ministry leaders in their luxurious lifestyles! In return, congregants should make sure the House does not lack, using wisdom to determine how to support. God honors and accepts the offering of an individual that gives from his or her capacity (he loves a cheerful giver), rather than giving from aggressive solicitation or demand!

Why do many ministry leaders burden their congregations and ministries with their own personal finances? Is it the obligation of congregants to do so? We as congregants understand that the man or woman of God has to live too, but what determines how much is too much and how much is too little? From my understanding, if a pastor is hired into an already established ministry, he or she receives a salary determined by the clergy or trustee boards of the ministry. If pastors desire to elect their own ministry foundation (start their own churches), they can structure the ministry as they choose, living right out of the offering baskets if desired—which is unwise and illegal!

How are we to determine what are necessities for our leaders and what are surely luxuries, which we know pastors can do without? In one of my former churches, the Bishop mentioned his children being high maintenance as they prepared for college. This was used to pressure the congregation to now begin providing college tuition for the pastor's children. Many congregants can't even afford college tuition for their own children, so how is it we have to begin affording this and other kinds of requests for our pastors, ignoring our own household needs?

There should be some other authority validating necessities, but when pastors establish their own ministries, it's tough to tell them what to do with the money! Would the ministry's money be considered the Pastor's? It shouldn't be! I would hope ministry leaders that have established their own ministries, would structure it in a way that the ministry isn't surviving from the pockets or pocketbooks of the owners!

Paul in the book of (II Corinthians 11) spoke about these kinds of situations, as he chose to evangelize receiving pay from churches, not being a burden to others. Many pastors choose to do the same, as many cannot live solely on what the church pays for salary, therefore electing to accept engagements (evangelizing), therefore to increase their annual income; the same as working a second job! When pastors find themselves being a burden on the ministry, it's time to get another day job, second or alternative employment, reaching out for addition preaching engagements, develop some product or start eliminating some of your expenses that you believe you need to afford!

Increasingly, when our leaders find themselves desiring additional income, their first thoughts are to "just get it from the people!" That should NOT be the first objective when our leaders find themselves in situations necessitating additional money! This behavior causes many to become very careless with the finances of the ministry, and this practice is becoming very common. This behavior can also lead our leaders to involve themselves in illegal activity, disguised as ministry operation, knowing that the ministry is operating way above its means. Other eyes should determine what is relevant when observing aspects of what a ministry refers to as necessities. You'll immediately find that ministries are outsourcing too many endeavors that can be utilized internally, perfecting the House.

Are you robbing God? Isn't this the famous congregant leather belt-beating statement? Then followed by (Malachi 3:10) used for scolding! Well, don't feel that way because our ministry leaders should tell us this, but rather should encourage us continually regarding God's Word concerning this matter! Just as there are many that didn't understand why we should bring an offering, there are those who still don't understand about returning the tithe. I know we sit week after week in our sanctuaries, but that doesn't mean we're being taught properly. Many times we're just told to do several things and then we're chastised when or if we don't comply!

There is a history of why congregants should return tithes to the Lord! It was customary among ancient nations to give a tenth of the spoils of war to the object of their worship. Although, we don't worship objects (praise God), it should be customary for congregants to give a tenth of our income to God! In ancient days, tithes were paid to Melchisedec as the Priest of the Most High. Some still wonder if the name Melchisedec is actually a name or a title since the Bible doesn't list any ancestry of his parents, or his birth and death. But Melchisedec is a character in Bible history that was both King and Priest, identified in (Hebrews 7:1-2). Melchisedec, many could say, was a type of Christ, so that Christ could be made a priest after His order, as Jesus Christ is also King and Priest!

What does Melchisedec have to do with me paying my tithes? All I know is Malachi, and he didn't say much! Many congregants have mixed understanding about what the Scriptures say regarding tithing. Often we believe that (Malachi 3:10) is the only place where the Bible speaks or teaches about Tithing. In the book of (Hebrews 7:1-10), the author teaches that tithing was not from the law. The Scriptures tell us that Abram, the first and most honored of all God's chosen people, gave Melchisedec a tenth of the spoils he took from the Kings he'd been fighting. This offering of tithes was an act of homage, reverence, subordination, love and faith. This teaches us as congregants that tithing is an act of an individual who responds with worship and reverence to God! When we return tithes and offerings to our Most High Priest (Christ Jesus), our hearts should be expressing love and appreciation, giving continual worship. This is God's regular possession; it belongs to Him at all times. That's why we becoming robbers and thieves when we withhold the tithe!

Tithes and offerings aren't about our ministry leaders; in fact, they should be returning tithes too! Again: ministry leaders should return tithes and offerings just like congregants. Since our tithes and offerings are not about our ministry leaders, you may be thinking, how is the tithe returned to God? The answer: just as it has been done for hundreds of years; through God's people, through those that represent with authority and through His established institution, which is the House (the Church). I know what you're wondering why there are other kinds of institutions asking us to return our tithes to them? I won't discuss that right now; you have to read "The Fight for the Tithe" (Section 4.3)

Tithing is an eternal principal. It's not something that is going to just disappear, and it's what we should do, as it is a grace to return tithes. It helps us, as congregants become stable, spiritually healthy people! We shouldn't feel obligated to return tithes and bring offering to God; it should be your personal expression of your love and honor, not because the man or woman of God is reaching for his or her leather belt and getting ready to swing! (You know how that goes.) Whether you're the only individual ready to return tithes and bring offering, that moment is about you and God! It's not about how much or how little you return; it is about how the Lord has increased you to be able to present your gift! Don't get caught up with the latest trends of the House; you will lose your position being able to come boldly presenting an acceptable gift. Don't forget God has in the past and I believe He still does reject our gifts, presented before Him as offering for He knows our hearts!

Congregants should be aware that everyone that stands before us within the established institutions for receiving our gifts are not focused on worshipping! We should be well informed that many ministry leaders seek to compete, using gambling type methods during this time of service. Leaders sometimes make bets regarding how much money they can raise! This practice becomes typical, especially when there's a visiting preacher standing before us, receiving our gifts!

Our leaders sometimes begin to step in the way of how we should position ourselves for worship, when they place themselves in debt with God's gifts. What I'm trying to communicate is; behavior that is noted when preachers are asked to come for special occasions such as anniversaries, convocations and other type of conventions to raise money! If he or she has come to your function, raising ten thousand dollars, now your pastor becomes indebted to the visiting preacher to return that favor! Your pastor must raise the same or an even greater amount for offering, continuing a competitive cycle in regards to raising money! I'm sorry to expose this practice to you but for many years, while we as congregants are worshipping unaware, a game is being played right in front of our eyes.

Just as with other kinds of gambling and games, there are winners, losers, and many times sore losers! In some cases, ministry leaders who have lost these kinds of bets have become threatened! Now having a debt to repay, regarding not being able to raise the same or larger amount of money during offering! When our leaders use God's gifts for gambling between assemblies, this allows the enemy to enter, interfering with the premise of our worship to God!

So the next time you're wondering why your favorite preacher hasn't returned to your assembly, there could have been foul play behind the scene, which you never knew about! In addition, leaders have been known to steal God's gifts, utilizing them for personal reasons, including the actual theft of preacher contributions that were collected for a visiting preacher, as this practice is becoming common as well! When a visiting preacher comes to your assembly to minister the Word, many times there is a separate basket during offering. Increasingly, the total amount of the visiting preacher's offering can possibly be higher than the actual offering received for the House. Therefore, trustees have been known to take back some of the money, submitting a compromised amount to the visiting preacher as a love gift!

It's now time for us as congregants to begin an investigation don't just sit back and soak up everything you hear! There is a lot of corruption in our assemblies, but if we desire to get the House back in order, or in order for the first time, we have to first get ourselves in order, then peacefully making sure others are doing the same. Just as it's dangerous for our leaders to play with God's gifts, it's the same with us as congregants. It becomes tragic when we withhold from God, for every occasion of circumstance from the Bible days to this present day has occurred when men and women rebelled against the order in which He has established! None of us are exempt from His principals and His established order! We as believers had nothing to do with the establishment and we can't change it; it's purposed by the Kingdom and that's how it will operate, whether we like it or not!

2.2 Money and Prophecy Lines

The restructuring of worship services has become the trend in thousands of ministries regarding what is known as receiving an offering. Ministry leaders for many years have taken slander for what is known to some as Money Lines. The practice is when an individual who proceeds to take up an offering requests specific amounts of money! Ministry leaders typically have a set amount of money (desired budget) to obtain, soliciting congregants to form lines, having specific dollar amounts in hand, represented in each line. The authority conducting the offering will target the House, asking for a certain number of people to form a line having the largest amount in hand. This line or other lines may form, asking for smaller increments of money. If the authority starts with a higher amount, those that may not have it must wait until they get down to their in-hand amount in order to give offering. Most times, small amounts of money are not accepted in money lines, as the authority will most likely conduct a freewill offering, after making sure there are enough people in the lines covering the desired budget! (You know they stand there counting the people while crunching numbers in their heads.) Lines can range from today's popular minimum of twenty dollars and soar up to even one thousand dollars!

This practice has proven successful for thousands of ministries, but has done disturbing damage to the lives of many congregants! Congregants feel as if they no longer have a choice in what they've known for years as freewill offering, as they are instructed to give what is being asked. Although ministries, which utilize the structure of money lines, their motive is to quickly obtain their desired budget(s), without having to come up short depending on congregants giving freewill offering!

Congregants still choose not to participate in these lines; I remember many years ago attending services in Brooklyn (The Borough of Churches), the place where I was initially exposed to this practice, and it instantly turned me off! I remember it always taking up so much time, and I never had the desired money being asked! Therefore, I did not wait until they got down to the amount of money that would be considered freewill offering; I would just stand in any line that would represent the amount of money I would give, if I had it! Ministry leaders have now begun restructuring how they conduct money lines, as many congregants are doing what I have done many years ago. Leaders are now beginning to request to see the actual money before you place it in the offering basket or on the tables. Some will even dare to request that you place the money in their hands to make sure you are actually giving money! I guess many congregants have begun filling out empty offering envelopes while standing in the highest money line; and doing other practices to avoid the embarrassment that now filters throughout many congregations during offering!

I've observed many leaders placing extreme pressure on congregants while conducting money lines. Many times congregants just don't have the money; therefore, leaders will begin using scenarios to market the things of God, creating an influential atmosphere (power of suggestion) making us feel guilty for not giving! This manipulative influence forces congregants to begin paying for God's grace! Most scenarios used are targeted toward free elements of the Kingdom, making us feel as if we're taking advantage, and then soliciting us to give out of guilt toward what is free of the Lord! Congregants then begin moving quickly to give an offering, as leadership will continue pressuring the House as if we're trespassers utilizing God's provisions without paying!

As societal measures continue to affect millions of households, whereas many families have set budgets of how much money they can afford to spend. This has now placed limitations on ministries, whereas congregants are finding church to be a major expense! *They run mental scenarios on you to get you into the lines who do congregants call when pastors and/or leaders are out of control?*

Congregants have been known for many years to not meet personal financial obligations, instead affording progressive trends of their assemblies. As mentioned earlier, there are many stories of congregants giving money set aside for their bills, mortgage and vehicle payments, and rent! This type of behavior seems unwise, but congregants have found themselves experiencing eviction, foreclosure, repossession, and bankruptcy, as well as other hidden financial and personal hardships! Many times when congregants get home, realizing they've given money which was set aside for other things, now not having any money to possibly maintain needed necessities! This kind of manipulation then places congregants in jeopardy, causing some to participate in illegal activity and other unwise practices to sustain themselves until their next payday or until their situation possibly change. When congregants find themselves caught up in situations generally not initiated by their own motives, there is no way they can later accuse a ministry! Many become very upset with themselves, not realizing what has been happening for so long, believing there is another force/craft working behind the structures of money lines!

When leaders begin to conjure scenarios used to implement a money line, they're typically executed very timely! A leader would simply look like a fool, jumping up at any given point during service to solicit congregants to begin forming lines out of nowhere! Leaders know there are specific times when a congregation appears to be open and receptive to offering. Just as a professional fisherman knows the best time and places to catch fish, ministry leaders are training themselves for the best time and places to fish for our money! Typically, money lines are best executed when there appears to be an escalated level of worship. It's the same strategy used in sales, when consumers are taken by surprise by a sales representative choosing to catch us when we're not really paying attention. The motive is to get the giver focused on something else; then proceeding to request money, in conjunction to our needs.

What I'm saying is; if a ministry leader can get us to begin focusing on some things that are lacking in our lives; continuing to focus us into all the diligence to stand strong, he/she can then solicit our giving in conjunction to how we need God for help; this then places a transaction on the Kingdom! Ministry leaders are increasingly utilizing the marketing of biblical principals as the major scenario used when implementing a money line or seed offering!

This structure can become very time-consuming, as ministry leaders are very adamant, even aggressive, regarding obtaining their desired budgets. Some will even walk their sanctuary aisles looking for individuals who appear to have money! I've even observed some calling out names of their congregants, as to pressure them to quickly move out of their seats to give, stating how they should be quick to believe, as if waiting or not giving is wrong! I can still remember many of them saying repeatedly, "We'll wait on you; you need to trust God with your money," "Is there anyone else that needs to step out on faith, believing God for your miracle, believing God for what he's about to do for you and your family." I can go on and on regarding scenarios used to solicit congregants to join a specific money line.

Why would a ministry leader choose to use a prophetic gift to raise an offering? Is this practice a common move of the Spirit, or is the motive behind it solely transactional? Utilizing a prophetic gift to raise an offering adds another level of controversy and speculation to congregants paying for the Word! "Thus sayeth the Lord…" has moved many into doing things which were not true utterances from the Spirit, but purposed from the individual having his or her own way with the people!

Prophecy lines are the most time-consuming verses the call for a money line. Money lines typically targets congregants having specific dollars amounts in hand, helping leadership determine, or rather meet, desired budgets. As prophecy lines creates the same transactional premise, but leaves the giver with an alleged Word from the Lord! Many times, leadership runs into problems when trying to give individual prophetic words during offering, as many congregants desire to give during this time! Therefore, to alleviate long lines, the man or woman of God speaks a general Word over the House, which becomes the transactional platform only for those who desire to give according to the delivered Word! The practice appears almost like gambling, as if there is a specific prize offered as contestants choose to play or not! In this case, the spoken Word would appear to be the prize (if it comes to pass), and your giving would determine your effort to win! This practice has been reformed and is better known today as a seed offering, soliciting congregants to now sow into the prophetic Word deliberated over the House.

Psychics and mediums fully utilize transactional forums for individuals desiring to pay for readings and foretelling. These arenas have been around for centuries, as it's widely acceptable around the world! Divination has been and still is forbidden in the Body of Christ, being a complete offense to why The Father has sent the Holy Spirit to dwell in the lives of believers, so why are we finding more and more Christians soliciting the help of psychics and mediums?

Christians are increasingly beginning to lack the knowledge of the Holy Spirit, even His functions for the life of the believer! Our sanctuaries are becoming more business-oriented, which creates an atmosphere that surrounds around our ministry leaders, whereas congregants have taken their focus off of the Holy Spirit! The mentioning of the Holy Spirit has clearly become just a terminology to many congregants, not realizing that the Holy Spirit lives in us to continue the work of Christ Jesus! That's why we have

His Spirit, because He desires us to turn over the harvest! We are good ground, as we possess the same power that raised Him from the dead, continuing His work to enlarge the Kingdom! Not utilizing His Spirit that dwells in us handicaps us in regard to His leading! Within that stage, you won't know the difference between a vampire and a prophet!

Psychics and mediums possess the same kind of gift as of prophets and prophetesses, as they retain the choice of how to use the gift. Either the gift can be used to bring glory to God, or it can be used for alternative motives! Christians should never invite the operation of divination into our lives! It immediately offends the Holy Spirit and then exposes our own psyche to other spirit leadings that are not of light but darkness! What a psychic may tell you will most likely appear true, as they are able to utilize their gift (if they really have one) to connect to some information regarding your life. But their trick is to allow the spoken words to disconnect you to the way of the Holy Ghost, which is purposed and already written! Jesus said *He is the door and all others that come are thieves and robbers...* (John 10:7-10). This clearly tells you that others will come, speaking a Word, while trying to lead you, deceiving, but are really stealing while ambushing your soul! The Holy Spirit is the only power source that a believer should ever seek! Everything else will only supply limited resources and ultimately get a believer stuck where he or she doesn't belong!

When utilizing a prophetic gift during offering, it then places an advantage on the man or woman of God receiving the gifts. As our society grows more and more compulsive, many congregants will begin paying for the Word increasingly! Therefore, as compulsive society grows, congregants are less likely to understand or read the Word of God for themselves, but depend solely on the ministry giving interpretation! Therefore, as a sign of gratitude or to say thanks, congregants will begin placing transactions based on what they have supposedly received! This behavior can then confuse a leader as now; he/she is made aware that congregants are willing to pay! When ministry leaders are made aware of congregants giving more money, some will try maximizing their potential, incorporating the forum into their assemblies!

Congregants must be very careful while in the presence of a ministry leader utilizing a prophetic gift during offering. There is always speculation involved, as congregants have experienced deceptive behavior without understanding how to pinpoint the cause! Many have fallen for the known alleged prophetic utterance: *"In Seven Days..."* including, *"Tomorrow about this time...."* These known scriptural–based slogans have captured emotions of thousands, possibly millions of congregants, then placing a transaction in the House. (Many of us have fallen for one of these at one time or another.)

When these kinds of false utterances don't come to pass, there isn't anyone to call with hopes of getting your money back! Churches don't operate like a retail outlet, whereby dissatisfied consumers are able to return an item to receive a refund. There is no way a man or woman of God is going to return your money for a Word that didn't come to pass! Even if a Word that is seemingly specific to details in your life is delivered, it's never wise to then place a transaction, as God only requires your faith and obedience! Most times the Word had been delivered from a visiting preacher, because he or she knows how to work the House, playing the hit and run game (raise money, get paid and go)!

In the Old Testament of the Bible, we find manifesting angels, kings, judges, prophets, and priests being the primary mouthpieces for the Kingdom. Continuing we have Christ Jesus, which called the disciples, transforming into The Apostles, then being positioned as mouthpieces. Jesus then advised that He wasn't going to leave them comfortless, as the Father will send the comforter, the Holy Spirit! When the Church was established on the day of Pentecost (Acts 2), we then became witnesses, empowered by the Holy Spirit, collectively becoming mouthpieces and other functioning members for the Body of Christ!

The utilization of prophecy shouldn't price tag the Word, wherefore congregant's today desire more and more to afford God's lips! The believer already has full access to His lips, now being able to come boldly to the throne room reflecting His characteristics, power and wealth, having already received The Kingdom, which resides within us, because of the purchased possession that has been received!

Is it okay to give money to the House for a prophet/prophetess to speak a Word about your life? Well, you may be surprised to learn that many are hired for this specific purpose! Even in the Bible days, kings would solicit prophets to come into their realms, prophesying over the people with motives for manipulation; using the utterance having alternative motives over the people! Generally, congregants today begin growing weary of their own leaders at times, as they say the same things repeatedly. Therefore, many ministry leaders will invite someone else to speak about the same thing, causing people to then move earnestly, giving as initially desired!

Prophets and prophetesses are increasingly solicited to prophesy over thousands of assemblies around the world! Many ministry leaders know there to be great response and diligence from congregants! It's extremely difficult to know the difference between a prophet and/or prophetess that has been solicited by our leaders and those who are the real mouthpieces deliberating from the Kingdom. They are sometimes coached before services, and many are specifically told what to speak about! Specific congregants are targeted with motives to manipulate or control, obtaining money or other kinds of payoffs!

In more general scenarios, they're solicited to help ministry leaders with fundraising, congregational growth and other areas, as the ministry desires to comb the House for every dollar and cent they can find! Of course, not all ministry leaders are utilizing prophets and prophetesses for these reasons, and many clearly utilize them for edification for their assemblies, as well as other spiritually based festivities for assemblies. Many congregants today are still not aware of how our ministries leaders in the Body of Christ are solicited to speak over or into our lives as believers!

Prophets and prophetesses should be very cautious of how they're using their gifts as well! There is great responsibility to the one that stands as representation as a mouthpiece of God! Many churches and political officials are increasingly seeking to purchase this tool as a way to manipulate or control! Prophets and prophetesses should use several determining factors when solicited to speak or deliberate at events, therefore not getting themselves caught up in hidden platforms for deception! It is known that many are threatened to speak with specifics in conjunction to being financially supported by a particular ministry, private party and/or business entity even their own congregants trying to manipulate their own leaders! If or when prophets and prophetesses choose not to comply, he or she risks losing financial support proposed or already given! Most times the financial support comes before the proposal as a type of bait to capture the prophet or prophetess who is willing to engage in these kinds of practices! This is also used to control the leverage of what is specifically spoken, as this will schedule how often it's done.

THE PRICE TAG

So again I ask, is it okay to place a transaction (give money) for a prophet or prophetess to speak a Word over/into your life? Many will try backing this with Scripture found in the Old Testament, as individuals sought prophets for direction, such as when Saul and his servant were looking for his father's lost donkey (I Samuel 9:6). In the next verse, you'll find Saul asking his servant what they should bring Samuel for giving them the direction they were seeking in hopes of locating the lost donkey. Many then use Saul's question as to further explain the need to bring the prophet or prophetess an offering soliciting help! So is it the congregant's initial motive deciding what to bring the man or woman of God when we're seeking help or direction? Of course this kind of practice cannot platform in our church sanctuaries, as congregants would definitely feel as if they're now paying for the Word! But there are prophets and prophetesses who have their own private practices where desiring individuals seeking help pay money for their services.

You will read by verse 9 (of the Scripture) that the servant had a piece of silver and told Saul that he would give it to the man of God in exchange for being told the way of the lost donkey. What is very interesting about this Scripture is that before Saul or his servant could make an exchange or even an initial introduction, Samuel (The Prophet) told them that his father's donkey had already been found! From my experiences God always speaks first, as Samuel already knew that he would run into Saul and his servant, because God had already spoken first!

I've had the same experiences in my life, having received prophetic utterances since the age of sixteen! I've discovered that I'm more open to receiving a Word from individuals who know nothing about me versus someone who has retained some information, desiring to speak a Word! This is solid evidence of the spiritual gift of Word of Knowledge. Many congregants don't know the difference between the spiritual gift of prophecy versus Word of Knowledge or Word of Wisdom. Trying to explain each function would make this chapter unbelievably long; therefore, I suggest you visit a Christian bookstore to educate yourself concerning spiritual gifts. You'll then be surprised how we're using them against each other as Christians, being ignorant of their real/initial investment!

In closing of this section, I'd like to say that many congregants are not taught effectively regarding the functions of five fold ministry and the functions of using spiritual gifts; therefore, we're vulnerable when leaders stand against us with hidden motives! We cannot continue to blame our ministry leaders for not educating congregants regarding changes now implementing our sanctuaries. The less you know, the more they can manipulate your thinking!

Restructuring will always take place, as congregants are typically never in control of these kinds of things. But I pray that congregants begin collaborating, making sure those who are present and those who are coming will never experience an ambush of deception in the House.

It all may appear to be a great move of God, but it can quickly take you by surprise deceiving you. Many believe the world is growing darker and more evil by each day, but I personally believe it's not the world, but the hearts of people. We can see the world as it changes from season to season and from day to day, but the hearts of people can take a very long time to uncover. That's why God looks at the heart, and it should be our prayer that He continually searches our hearts!

My brothers and sisters, God has clearly blessed us all with spiritual blessings, and we have to use them wisely. We don't have to afford His attention or pay for His provision; He is always mindful of us. There isn't one time or moment between earth and the

Kingdom when He's not thinking about His people! We're always on His mind, because Christ Jesus is still away preparing a place for us, that where He goes we will know, and guess what; He's coming again to receive us unto Himself! So stop paying for what you believe will bring you closer to Him you are as close as you can be at this point, until He draws you closer. The closer you get, the more you'll realize that your nasty legal tendency (money) means nothing to Him!

2.3 The Seed Offering
(Sowing into the Word)

What is a seed offering? Would this be a type of offering where congregants are able to sow and plant with hope of reaping a harvest? I don't find this kind of offering throughout Scripture so I'm wondering if it's something new. I can't tell you how many times I've been solicited to give a "Seed Offering" into a specific outreach ministry or church! Solicitation was generally used to encourage believers to sow into a specific doctrine as a symbolic act of receiving the spoken Word!

May I ask another question? What would be my seed, if indeed I desire to sow? Would it be legal tender (money), sown in agreement as a symbolic act of receiving the Word? How could money be seed? Or rather, why would money be seed? If indeed money were seed, what would be soil? I'm sorry to sound like a third grader, but I need to be sure we understand the premise. Would soil be the House, which generally is the administrative forum operating as a ministry? Or would soil be the man or woman of God receiving a seed offering? All of these questions are valid in trying to understand why congregants are now being solicited to sow into the Word as a symbolic act of receiving!

To my surprise, I've found this doctrine to be false! I discovered this practice being another scenario now implemented by hundreds of ministries, trying to get money from the people! I know you're asking yourself how this doctrine could be false, as many ministries have been doing it for years. Congregants still don't understand that we must begin reading the Word of God for ourselves! I'm not saying to disregard our ministry leader's teaching, but to further study and meditate on the Word, if indeed it was the Word! I understand we don't typically question our leaders in these aspects, as we consider them to have studied efficiently, being able to adequately minister accordingly. Congregants don't necessarily desire to fact check what the man or woman of God is teaching.

Jesus taught us that the "Kingdom of God is as if a man should cast seed into the ground" (Mark 4:26). This spiritual law is designed for believers who desire to sow with hopes of reaping a harvest! So again let me ask you, what would be seed? Would my seed be money, sown into the offering as soil, therefore utilizing this spiritual law and obtaining a harvest? If so, may I ask if you have ever received a harvest from this practice? I know what you're thinking: you're still waiting for the harvest. It's on its way any day now for God is going to bring forth your harvest. How long have you been saying this? Rather, how long have you been waiting? Also, how many other seeds have you sown during offering? Furthermore, how many times a month are you solicited to sow into the Word, and how often are you reaping a harvest to make you want to keep up the practice?

I'm not trying to confuse how you're giving money and your faith toward reaping harvest. I'm trying to encourage you to search within yourself, primarily getting back to what the Word of God has to say, regarding the Kingdom's way of operation, which sometimes isn't the same as our churches! Just a friendly reminder: your money can never be seed! Legal tender (money) possesses a nature that can cause corruption, but the Word of God is incorruptible seed! So, what are you going to use for seed if you're not using God's Word?

His Word only is seed for harvest, and the hearts of believers, as mentioned earlier, is only soil for seed! We as believers turn over the harvest as we continually nurture the Word/Seed in our hearts! We nurture this by what we say out of our mouths! Either we will continually speak things of life nurturing the Word/Seed in our hearts, or we'll speak deadly things, destroying the Word/Seed sown into our hearts! Utilizing God's design to nurture the Word/Seed in our hearts is the only way to reap harvest, as the Word is seed within itself! Our legal tender (money) is simply a tool for sowing, but not seed for soil. The principal has been twisted, placing a monetary focus on how we should give.

When our ministry leaders impart the Word of God into our lives, then proceeding to solicit congregants for a seed offering, it's not wise nor is it Kingdom principal for us to begin reaching into our wallets and purses affording the Word! Again, your money is NOT seed; it has corruptible nature because it's of this world. But the Word of God itself is your actual seed, for its incorruptible! I know you're probably wondering how this works because for years thousands, possibly millions, of people have been sowing their money into the House, waiting for a harvest! How do believers sow? We sow by our deeds, using tools to implement the process. It's the same process used in agriculture; individuals choose the right season and location, utilizing the right tools to prepare soil for seed! This is the same strategy you can use understanding how the Holy Spirit will direct you when, where, and how to sow! That's why I asked earlier, if you have ever received a harvest when implementing the practice.

Honestly, I have never received a harvest from giving money into a seed offering. I cannot tie back reaping harvest by one specific time giving into a seed offering, but I can tied back reaping harvest from deeds that I've done and/or participated in which I couldn't have been able to do without nurturing the Word of God in my life. I've asked others the same question, and they haven't received any harvest either! But what I have witnessed is that ministry leaders will always tell you the harvest is on the way! They keep telling us repeatedly, still soliciting us to give continuously. This then begins to discourage many people, as you begin feeling nothing is going to happen, but they still have to tell us or rather encourage us that God is faithful. Yes, we know He's faithful and we know and believe He can do all things! We're not taught that God cannot harvest what His Word/Spiritual law doesn't permit. Many times our leaders block the opportunity for God to manifest His Word, and other times, we ourselves block opportunity for manifestation of harvest!

When you desire to sow by utilizing God's principals for harvest, it first requires your faith, not your checkbook, credit card, or currency. If your ministry leader preaches on the 23rd division of Psalms, then solicits the congregation for a twenty-three dollar seed offering, he or she is not operating using Kingdom principals, but has instead implemented a transactional atmosphere based on what was spoken! This practice is becoming increasingly common, as congregants are now affording supposedly symbolic numbers/amounts making transactions in the House!

We all have at one time or another, been solicited in this way, as leaders have begun price tagging the Word, having budgeted agendas for the House. What will begin to happen if every Sunday, the man or woman of God begins to price tag each sermon? God help us all if they decide to preach from the 150th division of Psalms, proceeding to solicit the House for a one hundred and fifty dollar seed offering from each congregant! The most ridiculous and rather hilarious seed offering solicitation I have ever heard of is when a ministry leader at a convention solicited every woman to sow a twenty-dollar seed offering with hopes of reaping a harvest of losing twenty pounds! You would think congregants would have been able to use enough wisdom, knowing these kinds of transactional-based atmospheres cannot move God to do anything that is against spiritual or natural law! But leaders are beginning to understand more and more that congregants are less knowledgeable to God's way of operation. Therefore, we have a long way to go, bringing awareness to congregants regarding how some of our leaders are positioned against us! Sad to say, thousands of women at that convention gave the twenty dollars!

We can't fully blame our leaders that decide to utilize the Word, having an alternative motive behind the Scripture, because congregants are continuing to afford these practices. This then communicates to our ministry leaders that we're willing to pay. When the man or woman of God delivers the preached Word, he or she then becomes a sower. The Word is seed for soil for the hearts of those who believe, but we must remember that Satan comes immediately to steal the Word that is sown into our hearts. He is able to steal the Word from us if we don't have a root in ourselves, meaning that when situations and circumstances appear contrary to the Word, which was received, we cease from nurturing the Word! In addition, he steals by attaching a transaction (congregants paying for the Word), which then allows believers to place their faith in the amount of money given, whereas this allows deceitfulness, lust, and other cares of the world to enter in and choke the Word, as it will then become unfruitful!

The most common scenarios used today to solicit congregants giving large amounts of money during a seed offering is to begin deliberating material possession such as cars, houses, money, and other external things, enticing individuals to give money! When congregants in ignorance begin reaching deep into their pockets, trying to place a transaction in conjunction to receiving, it then becomes an opportunity for the enemy to deceive, leading us into lust, causing congregants to seek material possession because a transaction has been made! It's the same practice within a department store; you buy something with your money and you expect to receive your merchandise.

The Kingdom of God doesn't operate as such. The spiritual laws of the Kingdom aren't based on commodity/asset transactions but on receiving with your ear (faith comes by hearing), nurturing the Word/Seed in your heart (continually speaking faith-filled words regarding what has been received), and God bringing forth a harvest of His promises (His Word, according to the will of God for our lives). Without utilizing this principal, there will be no harvest, but just continual transactional-based opportunities for you to pay for the Word!

Why would our leaders come clean with us about these kinds of things, as there is immediate gain for them when they receive our money? They have no choice but to keep telling us to *wait on the Lord for the harvest*, because they don't want to disappoint congregants about all the money, cars, houses, and everything else that may or may not be coming! They will continue to pump the House, getting congregants excited about what is supposedly coming; meanwhile, our seed is falling along paths, as birds are devouring our seed, even others falling on rocky ground, including being scorched by the sun (Mark 4). May I just ask again if you have truly received a harvest from this practice?

Again: the practice of sowing into the Word in my opinion appears to be a false doctrine! It's impossible to sow into the Word, as the Word is actually your seed! How can seed be sown into itself? Why would there be a need for seed to be sown into itself? But indeed, the Word is seed within itself, which then multiplies by its design! Congregants should no longer participate in this practice, as it doesn't line up with the Word. Although, many ministries are increasingly implementing this practice as a way for congregants to give during offering, sowing into the Word is impossible because the motive is deceptive!

The hearts of believers are soil; therefore, the sowing should be taking place within you! If there is no Word, then the soil cannot turn over a harvest! If there is no soil, the seed cannot be planted for sowing! I'm not speaking in theory to say that the House should give you money, as I'm not talking about money right now! I'm speaking in regards to the spiritual law of Seedtime and Harvest; the principal established by the Kingdom whereas it works for the believer today! We have to stop thinking in terms of money being harvest, when it's time to sow or when we're in need! When the Word is sown into the hearts of believers (soil), it then requires effective nurturing! During this process, the believer begins to speak faith-filled words, which are according to God's Word (incorruptible seed), continuing the Seedtime and Harvest principal! Does this happen in three to seven days? Not necessarily. It can take months or possibly years, as the process will continue as God is giving increase!

Many congregants get discouraged when there aren't immediate results, believing God is an in-a-hurry kind of authority! But many times our ministry leaders communicate these kinds of transitions as well, leading congregants into rushing the process of reaping harvest. This then makes it challenging for congregants to nurture the Word/Seed, as it begins to choke what has been received. That's why many believers are not seeing results for what has been received! So then we develop a behavior of running from one ministry to another, trying to obtain new Word/Seed, not knowing there isn't a problem with the incorruptible Word/Seed; there is a problem with the heart of the believer!

How much Word/Seed can you actually possess and nurture at one time? Is it even possible for a believer to nurture a new Word every single week? How can we meditate and fulfill the requirements of all the things we hear (faith comes by hearing) on a weekly basis? Is that the faith that comes when we begin hearing? Does that give the soul the capacity of increasing as we begin hearing? I often wondered about this when watching televised ministry programs that extended product offers at the end of every episode. How much can we actually obtain, how much can we actually afford? We'll talk more about this later (read Section 4.1).

It's imperative that we as believers beginning examining and checking the seed before planting. I'm not suggesting doubting the Word, or believing the Word isn't true; for we all know that's impossible! I'm suggesting we begin to understand the purpose and destiny of our lives. What has harvested for Elder EDF isn't necessarily what God has prepared for you. Don't seek what others are supposedly receiving, as the Word that you're nurturing may even be greater or actually turn over something entirely peculiar!

Watch how you're nurturing the Word/Seed, as you should allow the Holy Spirit to lead you how to pray! You could be praying the wrong prayer; we know Jesus makes intercession for us, but we still could be praying carelessly. Don't pray what others have told you; pray God's Word over your life, because while you're nurturing the Word, it's still the task of the enemy to choke and destroy what you're carrying toward harvest. There are going to be problems while nurturing, but remember you will lose your seed if you don't have foundation. That's why the Word is seed within itself: you can use the same seed, creating foundation on what you're nurturing! The Word is all-powerful like that; it's incorruptible, and your money can't do that for you!

Why are you sowing in the wrong places? Why are you trying to purchase the outcome of spiritual law, instead of utilizing the soil that you possess every single day, which is the heart and Spirit that has been given. By now we've recollected the knowledge of giving and God's spiritual law. It really works when it's applied properly. I apologize for every ministry that has given you false information, leading you in wrong directions. Some of them don't know, and many of them only are doing what they've seen done. Many are watching Christian television networks, then implementing practices and doctrines as a means of improving their assemblies. But this can utterly stress the atmosphere of the House, as all assemblies are not on the same levels.

Doctrines and practices don't work just because we've seen them demonstrated; it takes our leaders strategically sowing into the lives of their congregants, as believers begin strategically nurturing the Word/Seed, as God awesomely delivers harvest through our lives! Its okay to examine the harvest to make sure it's according to God's Word. Many times, harvest had already come, but we've been busy nurturing something else. Have you ever had that experience? The process most times is continual because the Word is seed within itself; the outcome of harvest can continue for a generation, even multiple generations!

2.4 Sacrificial Offering, Vows, and Tainted Giving

What is a sacrificial offering? It appears congregants are asked to give sacrificially on a regular basis, not understanding the premise. Is a sacrificial offering something given when a church is trying to meet yet another target, asking congregants to give again into another offering? I don't know about you, but this terminology seems to be used frequently when our leaders are dragging out the offering, trying to reach their targeted budgets.

There is biblical history regarding giving a sacrificial offering, which is a type of freewill offering. Remember, a freewill offering is voluntary and doesn't stipulate specifics amounts when given, but is given out of generosity according to one's capacity! A sacrificial offering is typically given out of the abundance/capacity that a person has, whereas the sacrifice generally is given from the lack/poverty of the individual. In the Old Testament, a sacrifice many times symbolized something dead; it represented death from the giver, symbolized as a part of our desire or will become dead, giving life and substance to the receiver!

Congregants have to be very careful regarding what they believe to be a sacrificial offering versus freewill offering. Sacrificial giving doesn't permit one to invest in order to gain or receive a harvest or reward! This kind of offering primarily situates a giver to give from their lack/poverty, which then something dies; what dies you may be asking, our own desire including the area of abundance! When giving freewill offering congregants are able to give out of their abundance, without lack/poverty still gaining, as this positions the believer to receive from the Lord!

Giving sacrificially isn't required until you have self-sacrificed! Desiring something, and then sacrificing it for the sake of Kingdom building, rather than making us more comfortable, it's then turned over to others that need. So this means that if it's not going to bless someone else, you are not sacrificing anything! Therefore, we need to better educate ourselves regarding how our leaders are soliciting us for sacrificial offering. If your ministry leader frequently asks for a sacrificial offering, it's your responsibility to investigate the need. Every time the man or woman of God opens his or her mouth mentioning a need for this and that, it's not the congregant's responsibility to begin affording probable deceptive scenarios! You alone should determine whether your capacity allows you to give. A sacrificial offering is a type of freewill offering, so you can decide whether you desire to give. If you don't have offering to give, then a sacrifice may be applicable, but only after you've received validation/confirmation! The outcome of giving sacrificially should be to extend the Kingdom of God, or something or someone with virtue!

Your motive for giving sacrificially shouldn't be in expectation of harvest; your giving should be an expression of love (same for any kind of offering) to God, as you desired to sacrifice. Therefore, the outcome is that you've met the need of someone or something else, as it represented a cost for you. This then proves your love for Christ Jesus, who was given as a sacrifice for us, and helps us to grow stronger in our faith regarding giving! There is much biblical history regarding those who have given sacrificially, and congregants should further obtain knowledge regarding how the Lord would teach and show us when a sacrificial offering is applicable in our assemblies (II Samuel 24, II Corinthians 8, Luke 21, I Kings 17, I John 3).

What is a Votive Offering? Votive simply means fulfilling a vow in fulfillment of an oath or vow. Have you ever made a vow, a promise? In today's increasingly compulsive society, votive offering is generally formulated in our hearts, saying, "If God does this for me, then I will do...or not do this...for the rest of my life." Is this a good time to start laughing? Well, all jokes aside, there is biblical history regarding this practice as well. Why do we think we're the only ones that have run into foolishness or trouble? That's why we have the Bible; there are several stories and situations that unfold just like our lives we live today! (Genesis 28, Numbers 21, Judges 11, I Samuel 1, II Samuel 15). These scriptures give us biblical history that we're to pay our vows and not neglect them. This is a type of offering as well; as it should represent our expression of love to the God we claim we serve!

Votive offering seems to have vanished from our daily lifestyles, especially how we honor God in our sanctuaries. We have ushered in more non-historical movements, rather than maintaining our identity as believers. Votive offering in today's society is structured between God and ourselves, as congregants now believe God is open and available for bribery! We offend God when we approach the throne room with votive offerings that aren't real in our hearts. God rejects these kinds of offerings, for this is truly tainted giving.

The Bible also warns us regarding presenting false votive offering. It's always better that we refrain from making fleshly promises offered up to God, stating how we'll do something, and later failing to carry it out! When we begin failing, not fulfilling the oath, we've then offered tainted giving to the Lord. God isn't pleased with this behavior, for He knows our hearts and our motives before we even give! We serve a God who NEVER fails on his votive offering to us, His people, and He expects the same representation from us! This is a real relationship we have going; we're not in His hand just to take from His other hand, we're in His hand still being transformed more and more like Him. We can't be plucked out because He's still working on all of us! So stop taking from the other hand, trying to make the relationship one-sided, and allow Him to continue doing a good work in and through you; that will definitely prove classic for eternity!

There were times in the Bible where votive offering wasn't used to present a gift, an expression of love as used when offering any type of offering. There were times when the people vowed to cease from doing something until a certain time or event had passed. This symbolic expression is typically used to communicate to God a statement of "I will not...until the time/event/season has come..." (Numbers 6, Psalms 132, Acts 23). See how disciplined our biblical brothers and sisters were; we are so off track today! We can't even wait until the benediction has been completed, being in a rush to trample out the church doors. We have so much work to be done in our sanctuaries!

Why would God reject an offering? How does He determine which offerings are pleasing and which are not? In the Bible, you'll find there were times when God was pleased with worshippers' offerings and times when He wasn't, including some that even died offering strange fire (outside the design of establishment) before the Lord! What are God's feelings regarding our offerings today? I wonder what percentages of our offerings are pleasing unto God and what are not?

What our ministry leaders feel about our offerings are not necessarily the same thoughts of the throne room. Your pastor may feel you're one of the best members he or she has, regarding the amount of money you contribute to the ministry, but God may feel differently regarding your giving, being not pleased at all! This tells us that God's system for accepting our gifts are different from how our ministry leaders receive them. So again I wonder what is God's feeling regarding how we as congregants offer our gifts before him?

Unfortunately, our compulsive society represents money as an image worshipped before God! Therefore, when our money is used as an idol, God cannot accept it! This is a sure way to better understand how our gifts are possibly not acceptable before the Lord! You must remember that our tithes and offerings are not about the man or woman of God receiving them. In addition, when your ministry leader prompts the congregation to start waving offering envelopes in the air as a symbolic method for blessing or prosperity, it's the wrong motive! The giving of our tithes and offering is not a time to position us solely receiving, but giving; the focus is still worship! Nothing should change from the time before offering to the time it ends. Offering allows congregants to enter into another level of worship. *It is more blessed to give than to receive* (Acts 20:35).

Now concerning money/gifts used for worship, how are you generating your money? In other words, where is your money coming from? I know you're thinking what kind of question is this, possibly wondering what this has to do with how we worship. This question is very relevant to how we worship, for there were times in the Bible days, where individuals offered stolen and/or fraudulent items for worship before the Lord and were penalized! I told you earlier that some even died offering strange fire before the Lord compromising the ordination/establishment of how it should be conducted! So I'm asking everyone today, are you offering strange fire or tainted giving before the Lord?

I know I've stepped on some toes today, but we must begin understanding that our legal tender (currency) is of this world (corruptible), being used as our primary gifts brought before the Lord for offering! Therefore, my question is extremely relevant in regards to how we earn or possess our money. Not everyone that we observe giving money in our assemblies is giving honest money! I know this is a shock, but there are several sources of how individuals earn/possess/retrieve money, legally and or illegally. I'm troubling your thinking with hopes of focusing you to understand that we have placed too much faith in our legal tender. We believe money to do several things that we cannot accomplish ourselves, or primarily what we hope someone to accomplish for us. In some cases, you may be correct, but as believers we have to govern the way we use our resources by way of instruction of the Holy Spirit! For the Holy Spirit is the believer's instructor/teacher,

He is always available to help/assist us govern our finances and resources, having a balanced spiritual lifestyle!

The Kingdom has established the way in which we all must follow and/or comply. Everyone should give according to the established way of the Kingdom, and what's not based on that falls under disobedience, which causes hardship for us. It's always wise that we do things God's way, as all other decisions are categorized as sin! Therefore, when we try implementing foreign worship scenarios into our assemblies, it appears strange before God! A scenario used outside or in addition to God's system or design may lead congregants in the wrong directions. Many times, we as congregants believe trendy tactics used to receive offering are spontaneous moves of the Holy Ghost, not being aware they can cause your heart to lose focus of your worship! When your heart then changes, now, not being focusing on worshipping, you begin to taint your giving!

Tainted giving occurs when pride, recognition, and unwise or fraudulent giving takes place, including other elements, which begins changing the hearts of congregants! I can speak from experience, as this behavior can easily happen when you're worshipping in an atmosphere where a ministry leader begins to pressure the House. This typically becomes an issue during money and prophecy lines, including seed offerings. The motive then becomes one that will make you appear as if God is going to bless you more for giving a larger amount of money! Increasingly, congregants are offering gifts from resources that aren't necessarily purposed for giving, in my opinion! What I mean by this is; how can you give your child support money, rent and mortgage savings during offering, and then not be able to meet your financial necessities for living? This becomes an unwise practice, which congregants are increasingly continuing to do!

Our offering and gifts should be pleasing to the Lord. You shouldn't have a desire to steal or use fraudulent activity in order to render a gift to God! Why would you even desire to offer God something of that nature? Would He offer you something corrupted or tainted? Our mentality for what is offered and how we render our gifts to God has changed! This would be a good time for repentance, including a relevant time to begin praying that God search our hearts. None of us are exempt from the searching of corruption that may have crept into our hearts! Don't think you're the only one, or that I'm not talking about you; this is an area in which we all need to take the time and meditate regarding our old sin nature, as its designed to sneak up on us!

To close this section, remember that when giving offering, it's not about our ministry leaders! The focus is the Kingdom; it's about pleasing the Lord, giving from your capacity as your personal expression of love. It should be the same when giving freewill offering, returning tithes, giving sacrificial offering, including deciding how to resume disciplined strategies of giving votive offering. The next time the man or woman of God says, "It's offering time in the sanctuary," a true, real, Spirit-filled praise should flow from the core of our hearts, for this will clearly be the most personal time between you and God as you express an excelled level of gratitude. This isn't a transaction-based praise; this is a praise that should come forth boldly!

CHAPTER THREE

THE CHURCH

3.1 Order of Worship Changes
(Big Business/Less Ministry)

What constitutes a ministry a mega-church? Would it be the size of the congregation or the financial status of the ministry? How are we determining actual sizes of a ministry and/or actual financial leverages? Many ministries tend to shy away from discussing the details of their finances, as curiosity concerning this matter seems to be of great interest. Churches are always ready and available to boast of the size of their congregations, quoting approximated congregational membership.

There still appears to be an increasing number of individuals who feel mega-churches are becoming too impersonalized! Some believe they lack the ability to reach the needs of people effectively. Others disagree, feeling the design offers more opportunities for those who have specific needs. These types of ministries tend to have an overwhelming number of people, while some congregants' desire personalized attention, normally supplied by the actual pastor of ministries having smaller assemblies.

With increasing focus for outreach and missions, many pastors cannot personally meet with congregants who request one-on-one ministry; therefore, many ministry leaders tend to assign other leadership officials, designated in specific areas of service for congregants. Some still find this structure to be impersonal as well, still embracing the days when the pastor had an open-door policy. A pastor having an open door policy within a mega-church spells out heart attack and aneurism.

In today's society of increasing mega-churches, sanctuary worship services are changing with modern times. The traditional order of worship outlines are disappearing before the eyes of congregants. Testimonies, hymnals, choir robes, responsive reading of the Bible, observance of Holy Communion, Baptism, including the observance of yearly religious events such as Palm Sunday, are vanishing from the congregants' total worship experience! Many believe churches are now concentrating on big-business endeavors, including affording many luxuries, adding what they believe to be conveniences for congregants such as fast-food services, counseling centers, childcare facilities, and senior citizen housing! Many doubt the stability of these continually expanding ventures, but too many ministries are trying to accomplish identical goals! *They want you to get behind the vision, but they're all doing the same things.* Meanwhile, Debit/Credit Card impression have now made its way on offering envelopes, ATM machines are now in our sanctuary atriums and even automatic deductions are now being offered debiting congregant's bank accounts!

The stability of a mega-church cannot maintain operation having the traditional Sunday and midweek worship services. Therefore, congregants are now becoming overwhelmed with quarterly conventions, two to three midweek services, random revivals, concerts, and special calendar of events. These seemingly overwhelming functions aren't limited, as congregants are always solicited to purchase tapes; CDs, books, apparel and the traditional fried chicken dinner! Congregants are finding church a major expense! More services equals more money; the more invited preachers and special guests, equals the probability of more people; and more people probably equates to more supporters/givers, members and even partners!

Living with back-to-back scheduling demands now inflicted by ministry leaders, congregants are ordered to *step up on their giving*. This statement is used to encourage members to give more money, as many ministries cannot afford the capacity in which they're now operating! With monthly pledging and other activities of fundraising efforts to construct mega-churches, members are then pressured to pay off the newly constructed sanctuaries debt free (having limited to no mortgage), and you would think that after the scope of work has been completed, congregants would then be given a break. Not so! Congregants are then pressured to maintain all the ever-expanding ventures of the ministry! Congregants' finances are decreasing, as household incomes are not increasing! "We'll just get it from the people" is the most used statement when ministries are launching yet another venture! Are these ventures really benefiting members? Are these changes securing the stability of the ministry or flexing a muscle for the name of the House?

Overwhelmed by leaders abusing congregants with principals mixed with other motives, congregants are now beginning to feel the pressure! Twenty dollars today, ten dollars during midweek services, and then another thirty dollars on the following Sunday is now making a substantial difference in the pay structures of congregants! Living paycheck to paycheck or with over-limit fees, charge offs, and NSFs (non-sufficient funds) is an increasing part of the lives of thousands of congregants! *What happened to the true shepherds that God sent out to foot-wash the sheep?*

As I've carefully documented scenarios used to solicit the average congregant that would typically give fifteen dollars to now give fifty dollars is an interesting study! Congregants are not exempt from economic setbacks in today's society, as many feel they're now paying more than 10% returning the tithe and probably another 10% bringing an offering! Unfortunately, many ministries don't help support members in hardship and rarely supply any refuge (read Section 3.3). Feeling stuck under pastoral controlling doctrines, members are frustrated, angry, and depressed regarding still having no voice!

As recent days of churches seem to increase by the year, many pastors are growing insensitive to the common life experiences of their congregants. Societal challenges are changing household structures, including workplace environments, which can cause congregants to become unfaithful. Many try as hard as they can to maintain their loyalty, but become overwhelmed with unforeseen circumstances. Just as congregants structure their income to operate within a capacity for living, ministries can better manage and facilitate their incomes as well. Although, ministry incomes fluctuate weekly, there should be a base income used when factoring what a ministry can or cannot afford!

Operating from offering-to-offering, while trying to expand and grow a ministry may cause frustration among congregants. Where are congregants supposed to get the money? What congregants are doing to be able to keep up with church's desires can possibly be unwise or illegal. (Those are the stories no one would ever tell you.)

How are ministry leaders going to be able to maintain the stability of the increasing number of churches all doing the same things? Many will tell you repeatedly how the ministry is doing a unique work for the Kingdom of God, but when you begin investigating, you'll discover that predominately everyone is doing the same things. Many churches are beginning to compete with each other. Egos equating to operating in pride has now caused many to boast of what they claim God is doing for the ministry, trying to outdo what others have accomplished. Our leaders are competing in the rat race for whatever the prize may be, and congregants are suffering in the interim! Unfortunately, we as congregants have to afford these increasing changes now ambushing our assemblies, and we're pressured to maintain them, as pastors are adamant regarding upholding reputation.

When congregants begin withholding their responsibilities, leaders then become aggressive regarding failed and/or struggling ministry ventures. It's not the responsibility of congregants to afford every thing that the man or woman of God states, "God is now calling for..." It's imperative that we use wisdom and understand that many ventures our leaders are calling for are not beneficial or necessary. It may sound deep and spiritual when they ask, but give it a few days to rest on your heart, and you'll discover that the peace you thought you felt while listing to the solicitation isn't going to be the same!

Many times you'll have to meditate on how the Spirit would lead you. You cannot be quick and in a hurry to start funding everything that the man or woman of God is calling for! Remember, God is the one who sets the target for where He chooses to lead the House, if indeed He's calling the House toward a specific direction. Those who are spiritual will be able to pick up on His leading, as many times the Holy Spirit doesn't speak right away and definitely not at the same time our leaders are soliciting! Frequently, the Spirit of God has already been directing you in a specific direction;

therefore, when our leaders begin introducing a need to the ministry, most times congregants are already peaceful regarding giving into the offering!

Tune into what's going on in your spirit; focus on how God has been dealing with you in regards to your life and your family. You may discover how spiritually rich and wealthy you already are, without trying to afford the latest trends of the House. Many of these trends are not beneficial to congregants, as the designs are basically new products and/or other income based premises increasing financial margins for the ministry! Margins typically build and design beautiful sanctuaries, but after all the work is done, leaders will get back to the drawing board now soliciting yet another venture!

Why are there now so many ministries heading in this direction? Many of them discover that tactics and scenarios have worked for others, so this must mean its okay to implement the same strategy on their assemblies, pulling the people in the direction they desire. Let me warn some of you hustlers who want only to increase the financial margins of your ministry. You can possibly run into some major trouble trying to afford an unstable leverage. You may come up with a good sum for a targeted quarter of the year, but you may not be ready to handle the unforeseen debt that can actually land your ministry clean on its back when congregants begin withholding. What typically happens at this time is leaders then go full throttle with calendars of events, with the motive of offsetting the ministry's debt!

I don't want to display churches as pimping entities that are against congregants, as many are doing great things in and for their communities. Many have filled in the gap for under funded/budgeted programs that used to draw our local communities. Now ministries can offer the same kinds of services and programs that were once funded by their local cities, such as after-school programs, computer-training facilities, sporting complexes, and other programs and services that are beneficial for the local community.

Not only have these outreach endeavors improved what we believe about churches, but Sunday services have also become better atmospheres for praise and worship. Praise and worship teams have become more creative, integrating dramatic arts and eurhythmics into services, offering congregants an escalated level of worship. With these expanding worship additions, congregants still need to be aware that it costs money to maintain and operate these functions. Congregants still retain the right to choose whether they're willing to support these things for their ministry.

Congregational growth continues to be the primary focus of leaders, but setting order has to be priority as well. Crowd control, strategic house rules, parking lot safety, security, and many other aspects of facility services are in great demand, as congregants are becoming turned off when trying to make their way to and from church! What good does it do to boast of thousands of congregants attending your services when there is no order in the House? Some services start twenty to forty-minutes late and/or get out at unreasonable times, while some services are nearly four hours in length having another following.

Moreover, leaders must understand that not everyone who comes to church attends for praise and worship. The number of sanctuary complaints has now risen to an unbelievable number and includes a large number of stolen property reports. It's not enough for ushers to walk the aisles looking for congregants' chewing gum; they must be trained to walk the aisles looking for recording devices, snack bags, cigarette boxes and proper attire. If situations now affecting our sanctuaries don't improve, security officials may seek to implement bag screeners including the operation of metal detectors at sanctuary doors!

You may think I'm joking, but if things are out of order now, imagine if congregants or ministry leaders choose to disregard this message. Then I'll have to write another book about detention facilities behind pulpits, wounded bodies on undressed communion tables, next to empty baptism pools! We have to begin getting serious about the changes affecting our sanctuaries and our society. Many times, churches feel as if they're exempt from precautionary measures, as if a few security guards are going to help secure a large building. Congregants should be better prepared to know what to look out for as well.

Do you know there are a large number of people that target to get over on the Church! Sometimes we're even robbed from those that seem unfortunate trying to help, all the while; their initial motive is to take from the ministry! We understand operating in stewardship, meeting the needs of those that are in need, but there are a large number of individuals that know how to simply run sympathetic games on ministries! This makes it very difficult for our ministry officials to determine who really needs help. Many times congregants that are faithful to the ministry, even their tithers, are rejecting when in need, because the ministry has positioned itself not really knowing whom to help!

Big business is equivalent to big responsibility! You can't pray and seek God for large territory and then fail to be responsive to your existing ground. Millions of congregants may come and go, but what about the lives of those who helped build these facilities? Moreover, choir members, praise and worship leaders, musicians, and others contribute to make the House what it appears to be! So if you're a pastor thinking that you're the primary reason your ministry is operating successfully and that your sole purpose is putting butts in the seats week after week, you need to put this book down and fall to your knees to repent, for you are clearly caught up in yourself!

It takes hard work and dedication to be able to establish and maintain any kind of ministry. As financial margins increase, allowing our leaders to expand their ministries, there should also be compensation for those who serve (read Section 6.2). Ministry leaders shouldn't be the only ones taking home a salary. Half of the congregants probably came just to hear the choir. In fact, without them, I would be surprised if the church would be half full on a steady basis. Most times congregants are getting better Word from the lyrical content of their songs, than the man or woman of God standing before the people!

If a pastor wants to boast of its congregational size and financial leverage, it's now time to start operating like an entity that serves according to those realms. If this clearly is the direction for your ministry, you should strive to understand that you can't operate a business of this size like you did when you were probably a storefront! Congratulations to those who have progressively grown from a storefront to a larger church, which is a tremendous accomplishment, but as each realm of accomplishment gets higher, you must reorganize your internal structures. You have to strengthen your internal organizational foundation, as clearly this is where many problems reside. Additionally, you need to get many of your family members and friends out of the way, professionally employing verifiable candidates who know how to keep an expanding business in operation.

In closing this section, let me stress that I understand ministry leaders want to expand and grow their business, as I too am a business owner. I know the sacrifices it takes to get from plan A to plan B and then back to plan A to restructure and reestablish a business. But don't forget there are people around who commit themselves to helping us, just as pastors utilize their gifts when ministering the Gospel. It's time to stop implementing the strategies from the days of old, as we don't live in those days anymore. Their needs to be a new way to establish and maintain expanding ministries, and I hope this book will help leaders position themselves for change!

3.2 Materialism and Spirituality/Mentality
(Who's Really Prospering?)

The prosperity doctrine over the last seven to ten years has become the major trend when ministry leaders are seeking to expand or progress their ministries! The teaching has encouraged millions regarding God's design for wealth and success for believers. Of course, as with most things, there are positive outcomes and negative ones. The doctrine has become so contagious that many Christian bookstores have altered their finance sections, now shelving an overwhelming number of books related to financial success for believers. I was in awe visiting a Christian bookstore in New York City when I discovered the size of the section devoted to financial success, money and prosperity! I was searching for a publication that would give me historical information regarding the establishment of offering, including information about why congregants should return tithes; to my surprise, I found nothing!

When observing ministry leaders who choose to solely carry the message of prosperity, many are observed marketing FREE principals of the Bible such as healing, forgiveness, harvest blessing, restoration, and even reconciliation. This doctrine also has a partner in crime called the "Debt-Free Doctrine," which teaches and solicits congregants to plant/sow (money) with hopes of reaping a harvest of debt elimination and/or of being debt free! Supernatural debt elimination has become a major target, as congregants believe sowing into the teaching is going to move God to wipe out revolving debt or delinquent bills!

Today there are an overwhelming number of books, tapes and CDs such as the popular slogan *Money, cometh to me now!* (The wise slogan that has never made it to the mainstream is *the only way to become debt-free is by paying your bills*) Its unbelievable how many congregants apply this doctrine to their lives, believing they can escape fulfilling their financial obligations, such as credit cards, auto, and mortgage loans. *Why would God have to cheat a financial institution to back up this doctrine?* Congregants are obviously noticing that this doctrine increases profit margins of authors, preachers, and teachers only!

After diligent study, many are finding that the prosperity message has a double standard. Thousands or possibly millions of believers are frustrated regarding visible changes in their ministries, stating, "The only fruit we're seeing is the prosperity of the man or woman of God, telling us how prosperous they are!" Many enjoy larger homes, luxury cars, expensive apparel, exotic vacations, while many believers are now more in debt than before the prosperity doctrine! With the motive of outwardly demonstrating prosperous living, congregants have begun purchasing expensive items as well.

Believers have begun trying to demonstrate the outward appearance of living blessed; the doctrine, unfortunately, has triggered congregant's motives to outshine believers and un-believers! The motive has corrupted the hearts of believers, as non-believers tend to feel that church folks are only demonstrating ignorance regarding who God really is! Many times when speaking with un-believers, they desire more virtuous things of God than believers! Although, they are not ready to receive God as Lord, many retain an adamant passion for spiritual things verses believers!

Our sanctuaries are growing increasingly competitive and congregants are even trying to outdo each other. Many feel as if the sanctuary is now the place to showcase blessing and provision! Some feel it necessary to boastfully state, *Look what God has done for me!* As mentioned earlier in this book, you should be careful how you look at others who seem prosperous, as you don't know how they've obtained what they have. It's becoming common that congregants are not testifying honest and/or virtuous deeds demonstrating a holy lifestyle! It is known that many have created the outward appearance as it helps their esteem deal with several inconsistencies!

How prosperous are congregants when their bank accounts are empty with minimal to no savings, cashing in their 401k plans, etc., in order to obtain the favor of the Kingdom. (The teaching used to draw/solicit offering) This doctrine is increasingly growing limited through the eyes and experiences of thousands of congregants.

It is known that whenever you start talking about money, you can instantaneously gather individuals together; getting them to do things they never thought they would, even establishing a ministry. I feel this behavior demonstrates how the Gospel has become too Americanized! I apologize to congregants within other countries that we reach by way of electronic communication, demonstrating a compromised doctrine! Unfortunately, this is the mind-set of our society, and ministry leaders now desire to implement the prosperity doctrine into their assemblies. It's important that our leaders begin examining their motive to do so.

Unfortunately, there is no question that the Church community at large has been affected by this doctrine, having more of a negative outcome than a virtuous one. The influence that proceeds from pulpits has the authority to persuade congregants in either direction, yet many believe congregants can't blame their leaders! We serve a God that doesn't frown on those who first meet their financial responsibilities regarding tithing and offering, and then choose to purchase luxuries! The motive behind how congregants are choosing to spend money to purchase commodities/assets is what determines what is sinful and/or unwise.

What does prosperity mean to you? How does this doctrine or status of living define who you are as a believer? Does prosperity only mean money to you? If so, you have the wrong mentality for materialism and your spirituality will die! The Kingdom of God has greater fulfillment than what legal tender can ever offer you. Many times we become confused when our leaders are preaching about prosperity, thinking only about money and getting caught up in what our leaders have. We think we must obtain similar status. This is proof that our mentality has been affected, as we now desire to be like someone else!

The Bible teaches how believers should be prosperous, but what is God's direction for you? Have you even meditated on the areas of your life that God desires to increase? Your life as a prosperous believer has nothing to do with your leader and others around you. Our leaders preach prosperity to us to encourage us to bring more money into the House! God's design for prosperity in your life could transition you to leave your local assembly for another one. Don't allow your leaders to preplan what God is about to release in your life. Many will then place personal obligation on you, making you feel guilty if God chooses to do something different, outside their personal plans or motives.

As the prosperity doctrine will most likely continue to increase, having multitudes of congregants making wise or unwise decisions about how they spend their money, congregants should truly understand that materialism would definitely kill your spirituality! What's sitting in your driveway, lined up in your walk-in closets, or sparkling from your neck or arms, cannot compare to the prosperity of what God has prepared for your soul and spirit. We can't begin looking at individuals who drive luxury cars labeling them "worldly!" My definition of being worldly isn't anything outside of the church, for if you look very carefully; you'll most likely see the same aspects in both places! For being/living worldly has always been about your mentality! The way people think determines their destinations. The ways in which individuals choose to travel the course of their lives are rooted in what they think; listen to, and definitely in what we say!

There is nothing wrong with an individual working hard to fulfill his/her financial responsibilities and having financial discipline to achieve desired goals for wealth. But when the motive become boastful and prideful, then we can better understand their being another motive causing speculation! It's sad to realize that our leaders encourage us to look and exemplify a certain way as believers, and then we're criticized, even chastened, when we begin spending our money on things we desire. The first quarter of the year, we're hit with annual slogans for our sanctuaries, which supposedly identify a theme. Then, as we begin progressing into that direction, by the second quarter, we're beat up verbally regarding our commitment to God and/or other areas that contradict the identified theme!

Our leaders must begin to examine how they're treating God's people! You can't nurture the sheep today and then kick us out of the gate tomorrow (of course, after shaving off all our wool).

Many of our leaders are abusive, and congregants should begin documenting what's transpiring in their local assemblies. Before we become numb to the abuse, its time we develop strategies to better understand when destruction is present.

My motive isn't to advise congregants to cause commotion within their local assemblies. I understand that many of us get angry and seek God for temperance, but until you can peacefully address concerns, you are not exempt from taking a stand in the Body of Christ! If you don't care about what you're hearing or what is happening to you, change your mental position and begin thinking about those who will come after you!

Many of our leaders are only concerned about what we can do for them. They will continually strive for congregational growth, which eventually spells out more for them as well. As the focus is growing toward bigger business and decreasing ministry, congregants must retain their decision-making efforts. It's God desire for you to prosper as well! Giving all of your money to meet every goal that the man or woman of God is calling for isn't going to get you any closer to prosperity. You're going to find yourself later burnt out, broke, confused, and angry because you won't have any answers for your own behavior. Although, your leaders will continue to encourage you, telling you prosperity is on its way, which will quickly begin wearing thin.

Of course God isn't an in-a-hurry kind of God, but He can be when it's in His will to manifest provision. So I don't want you to believe that God doesn't honor your giving, if it's from your heart, given freewill; He accepts that expression and blesses you accordingly. But we can't look for money and other material possessions, believing that's the only way He provides for us. I know it feels good to obtain possessions, and it feels good giving them as well, but the exchange of material possession can change the heart of an individual, as your appreciation of such objects will eventually decrease.

If you always knew you'd get a specific material gift every time you've done something, your appreciation would not remain the same. That's why God doesn't give us a new car every time we give one hundred dollars for offering. He doesn't give us extra money every time we give sacrificially. God blesses us according to His will and by meeting our total need. Many times, we don't even know what we're in need of; therefore, when we pray, Jesus makes intercession for us. That is the perfect design because increasingly congregants are praying for all the wrong things!

When our leaders tell us about how God has blessed them with unexpected income, we cannot believe God is going to do the exact same thing for us. Our leader's income many times is from tax-free gifts and donations. Therefore, how can we begin comparing our economic structures when we typically work in taxable environments? If someone was to give us a large amount of money, we couldn't pocket the money and say, Oh, bless God. We have to consider that money taxable income. Non-profit organizations that obtain a tax-free authority are able to state income and expenses. Congregants have to claim all income from every source.

In a recent story about an Orlando, Florida, congregation, an investigation had taken place regarding the financials of the pastor and his divorced wife. During the divorce filings there was provided a list of the couple's assets, which detailed three Mercedes-Benzes, a Porsche Carrera, a Hummer, a Ford F-150 pickup truck, a Volkswagen Beetle, and two Harley-Davidson motorcycles; the congregation paid for these vehicles!

Shopping sprees, multiple mortgages, and escalated expense reports including other sometimes-undocumented transactions, ministry trustees are approving the expenses of many of our leaders. What commodities/assets should congregants pay for, and what types of expenses should our leaders purchase on their own? Should congregants be able to view the expense reports of our pastors? Should congregants determine if our leaders are enjoying luxurious lifestyles through the supports of the ministry? We've all heard the stories of luxury cars, private jets, five-star hotels and million-dollar mansions, but who is supporting these lifestyles? Should congregants continue to support their leaders on these levels, which exemplify success, image, and status, or should congregants withdraw their support, allowing our leaders to afford only the lifestyle drawn from personal income.

There is nothing wrong with living in the capacity of how God is providing for you! He has promised to teach us how to obtain wealth, and He is committed to do so as long as we seek Him for the direction. We as congregants are prosperous already, whether we have much or very little. God's Word is true whether we're living in a huge home or living out of public storage, whether we're driving a luxury car or taking public transportation. Don't compare yourself with what others have or by what others are doing! God works with us as individuals, knowing our specific need before they're even revealed to us, and He supplies them according to His riches. Our legal tender (money) is filthy (corruptible) before Him, for it cannot do what we believe in our hearts it can do.

Are you truly prosperous? What determines if you are or are not? Prosperity isn't leveraged by what zip/postal code you live in, nor is it determined by your lineage. An individual shouldn't be deemed prosperous based on having a college degree, owning a home, driving a luxury car, or the color of his/her skin. It's not about material possession; for those in other countries are prosperous without all the luxuries we Americans and other countries consider signs of being prosperous. Prosperity has always been about how an individual chooses to nurture the Word of God!

For the Gospel to be true, it must be applicable worldwide, which means it must work or be applied regardless of all the examples I've used in the previous paragraph. If and when believers nurture the Word of God in their lives, then they become prosperous. You could be a homeless individual with no assets and be a very prosperous individual! Many will disagree because of what society dictates regarding outward appearances. That's where we mess up regarding our mentality and we definitely mess up our sanctuaries!

You cannot begin labeling individuals as prosperous, looking for tangible aspects to place the individual into a certain category. My life has experienced much of what I used as an example, as I've become more prosperous not having the externals that individuals look for, then placing leverage! As I began to nurture the Word of God continually in my life, it led me in directions purposed, gravitating things that are of destiny! That is the most extraordinary Kingdom principal I've ever experienced.

As we nurture the Word of God, it creates manifestation of God's purpose for us on earth, as it is already written in Heaven! So if you're experiencing lack, or what appears to be poverty, start or increase nurturing the Word of God, and watch how it will gravitate and prosper your life! By doing this, many things you struggled to accomplish for years will begin to become easy, while other things will begin to happen automatically.

Don't forget that the life of the believer is soil for seed and the Word of God is seed for soil. External sources have their own system, which governs other principals for operation. If you desire to be prosperous, begin nurturing the eternal ever-increasing prosperous source, which is the Word of God! It contains no limit or boundary. Use it to defeat a situation which appears as poverty, as it only looks that way because God's Grace is sufficient and His strength is made perfect in our weakness. I'm not telling you this therefore an exchange of money being attached, as to what happens in our sanctuaries, I'm freely reminding you therefore we can begin getting on the road to the correct ways of obtain God's wealth and prosperity for His people!

We utilize the best system for making things happen in the world and that is the Holy Spirit. When you allow the Holy Ghost to nurture seed for soil in the temple in which the Spirit resides, things must multiply! Prosperity is an internal result first, and then it makes its way to the outward source according to the will of God. Let the work be done on the inside first, for when we dress up the outside, folks know we're faking it from the moment we speak if there is no foundation in the heart!

So again, I must ask you, who is truly prosperous? Many of our leaders are telling us how prosperous they are when they really are not that prosperous! If everything about them reflects an external/materialistic appearance, something isn't right with your leadership. This behavior then leads congregants in wrong directions, including making unwise decisions about how to spend their money. Get back to what God is calling for your life as an individual member of the Body of Christ; not disregarding leadership (oh no) but understanding purpose and destiny of your position in the same body! Things will work out peacefully, as you'll no longer be frustrated with the man or woman of God trying to obtain all of your resources for his or her own selfish desires.

I'm glad God supplied strength for me when I wasn't able to do it myself. Today I'm able to share how I continued nurturing the Word of God, while experiencing horrific situations in my own life. When life strips you of everything you think you have, let it all go, as you can't swim with a luxury car on your back! Remember to fight for your seed; for it's the only thing you need to be aggressive about. It will save your life, rebuild your structure, and restore you as if nothing bad has ever happened. People will look at you and say, "Isn't that the person who..." and never understand how you were able to stand strong, maintain your identity as a believer, still speaking faith-filled words. May our souls continue to prosper!

3.3 No Refuge

As congregants, we dedicate years of our lives and are devoted and committed to ministries, as it reflects the same expression for God! Many have supported their ministries during formation, making numerous sacrifices to keep the ministry operational, as new pastors understand that they cannot do it alone. Ministry leaders who form outreach groups require committed individuals who are able to get behind the vision and support the work!

Dedicated individuals are becoming overlooked, even though many have sustained their assemblies during rough periods and neglected their own personal obligations in hopes of pleasing the Lord. As the focus for conducting ministry is becoming more business-oriented, having decreasing ministry, our leaders are increasingly growing insensitive toward congregants and their supporters! Without congregants and ministry supporters, many struggle and are sometimes not able to maintain operation.

Should there be some kind of allocation for congregants when in need? If I'm not mistaken, I believe this is why we establish ministries! I'm not saying that a ministry's sole premise is to become a handout forum, but a ministry should be able to serve those in need. Many ministries are adamant about stating how they feed and clothe the homeless, but have you thought about your own congregants that sit in your assemblies week after week with needs of their own?

Why isn't there an established auxiliary within more of our assemblies to help congregants when they need it? Most congregants are told to utilize the assistance of deacons and other caretakers when there is a pressing situation. As our ministries are expanding into larger areas of outreach groups and supports, we must begin to restructure the way we believe the organizational foundation of these ministries should function! Congregants should be informed how the ministry can assist members when there is a need!

Have you ever heard of someone being rejected from his or her own assembly? You might be surprised to learn that this is becoming an increasing situation, as ministries are not meeting the needs of their own members. Even for faithful members, ministries are not prepared (having no resources, so they say) and don't really factor in supporting their own members when planning their outreach supports!

How can ministries outsource hundreds of thousands of dollars, even millions, on a monthly basis without allocating any funding for their own congregants who are in need? This lets us know that there is No Refuge for congregants who support the House week after week. No one can anticipate unforeseen situations and individuals may not have family or friends that can help. Increasingly, we're concentrating on demonstrating a prosperous lifestyle, which when there is a real need; individuals find themselves embarrassed to state their current situation. Therefore, we must get our sanctuaries back to having real congregants seeking and worshipping God!

When I was a member of West Angeles COGIC, there was time when I needed help, not financially, but regarding an approaching serious hardship. I went to a friend I knew had the resources to help me, and then I asked someone else who was a member of the same church for help and was declined by both people! My last resort was to look to the ministry for assistance.

I remember someone in the counseling center advising me that the division of the ministry was unable to help me because I didn't have a substance abuse problem. I couldn't understand why someone with a substance abuse problem would receive priority over someone trying to avoid approaching hardship. I would think it would be a faster process to help someone who is already able and functional, rather than someone with whom it could take years for results. I was discouraged that the ministry didn't have an outreach source for someone that wasn't down to the dogs, but at the same time still needed some support.

I was then introduced to a second individual who worked in another area of the ministry. I had to explain my situation in full and hoped that maybe this area could better understand my situation. To my surprise, I was asked a few questions that were basic but seemed to have a twist to them. First, I was asked if I was a member. As a member, I was able to give my membership number so the individual could locate my information on the computer. While the individual began pulling up my profile, I was asked if I'd completed new member classes. I stated that I didn't complete the classes because they conflicted with my schedule, but I'd been a member for years. I was then told in a nasty tone that I am "not considered a member!" I found this statement very offensive, as I'd been a faithful member and tither, even making a pledge toward the new sanctuary. I didn't think I would be treated like someone off the street seeking to get a hand out from the church. I thought that my membership profile would have demonstrated my commitment to the ministry and would have opened some kind of opportunity to help me avoid my approaching hardship.

THE PRICE TAG

This was when I change how I looked at ministries! Many thoughts quickly passed through my mind, as I didn't understand why I was being treated like a trespasser; after several times being told, "There's nothing the ministry can do for you!" I became very upset, not understanding how you can return your tithes and offering on Sunday, and then be told by midweek that the ministry can't help you! The individual left the office and returned moments later, stating that the ministry could give me two hundred dollars for public transportation to get around town (I guess to seek another source for help). The individual also offered to give me a piece of paper to take down to the Los Angeles City Shelter so I would be able to have a roof over my head in case I needed it! If indeed I desired to seek temporary shelter, why would my own church send me to the city shelter when they owned housing property? Why do congregants afford our ministries to purchase/acquire many things, but we cannot utilize them ourselves when we're in need?

By this time, I was already discouraged, not being able to comprehend what was really happening! I couldn't understand how a ministry that I'd supported for years could turn me away! I asked for my tithes and offering back, if indeed I was not a member of the church. Of course there was no way you can get money back from a ministry! As the individual handed me a check for two hundred dollars, I was asked to sign some paperwork and to pay the money back to the ministry when I was able! Still puzzled because I hadn't come to the ministry for money, but was seeking other assistance that could possibly help me save money to avoid hardship, I felt demoralized as I was handed something that really couldn't help me, but was appreciative of the ministry offering me at least something.

By the next church service, I returned the tithe right from the money the ministry had given me and then later that year paid most of the money back. Even today, I still can't understand how I didn't remain bitter for a long time. I don't believe that situation was to turn me against the ministry or churches as a whole, but it taught me a major lesson, encouraging me to write this book, to let the world know that our churches don't offer much refuge for their own congregants! Although, it has taken me several years to join another ministry, I still considered the West Angeles COGIC a church home!

Our assemblies should be in a position to help us when we're in need! In the past I've heard stories of members seeking help from their assemblies and being turned away, but it didn't make much sense to me until it was my turn to need help. These kinds of situations have turned people away from the Church. There's always reasoning behind why individuals refuse to deal with church and those who attend! When we begin humbling ourselves, understanding why individuals have chose to exempt themselves from churches, this will prove the necessity of getting our sanctuaries in order!

It wasn't until early 2004 when someone I knew had an experience with her ministry as well! Her situation wasn't similar to mine, just being a regular member of a local assembly; this individual was a leader in her ministry! It's a different scenario when you're a leader in a ministry needing help verses just being a congregant that no one really knows. I guess when you're a leader in an assembly, there is a certain attachment to the ministry, and leadership should seek to help you without question. What if you were the pastor's assistant and your spouse was a praise and worship leader? Do you think there would be some kind of urgency to help those that serve even you? Well, I must disappoint you

THE PRICE TAG

again, as some ministries are not in position to help those that even serve within leadership!

As mentioned earlier in the book, there was a major testimony given by the homeless married couple living out of their car. What was extremely shocking was that they were leaders in their ministry. It's unbelievable that leaders in a multimillion-dollar ministry can find themselves in these kinds of situations and not have someone to call! I'm pretty sure there is someone to call, but the question still remains why are congregants choosing not to utilize the sources that are established?

Congregants are discovering that our assemblies are now beginning to operate more and more like city services funded by the government! You would think your ministry officials would be compassionate toward members seeking help, but many of them are just as nasty and rude as government-supported agencies. You try to peacefully explain your situation while all broken up inside and you're interrupted with scolding that demoralizes you like a child. This is probably why most congregants choose not to share their personal situations with their assemblies! Let's not forget that it's not easy to approach someone you don't know when needing help, and many of us don't even approach our own family members. Why are the environments of our ministries structured like government, having the same type individuals making decisions over congregant's personal circumstances?

Government grants and other programs to sustain many outreach structures offered by our churches are now funding many of our assemblies. Don't let them fool you into believing there is refuge for congregants when in need, for these programs offered by your church are for individuals who have substance abuse problems, are ex-felons, are disadvantaged and others who seek long-term assistance. If it doesn't seem long-term, you most likely won't qualify. Long-term equals' longer funding, longer funding equals' expansion, and expansion equal more funding!

Don't be fooled when your ministry leaders boast of how God is blessing the ministry with all the programs that they offer! Many of these programs are additional income sources for your assembly! Many ministries are no longer solely dependant upon congregants' tithes and offering for the primary funding source. Ministries are diligently seeking for other sources to increase their margins. Many times, individuals associated with these programs are protected, because their long-term evaluations, occupancy, or treatment equates to continual funding of programs!

Don't try getting in the way of a ministry trying to seek government grants and funding, for you will definitely be moved out the way. Ministry leaders are becoming more adamant regarding seeking financial stability for their businesses—Oh, I apologize; I mean ministries! If a ministry loses its funding from the government, it's extremely difficult to get it back, as they're often times evaluated regarding compliance. Increasingly, churches are beginning to seek these kinds of financial backings, as tithes and offerings seem to have become limited!

Imagine what would happen if the government withdrew its funding from these programs, as they have with city sources in the past. How are churches going to sustain these operations when their income was focused on government funding? Congregants will have to afford these programs as well, because before a ministry ceases to operate a program, they will of course try to continue their funding through member contributions!

So again, is there any refuge for congregants when they find themselves in situations where they need help? Is your ministry prepared to handle situations that can ambush the lives of congregants? What programs/services are in place for congregants that find themselves in situations needing help? Is there any protocol in place so congregants can confidentially seek help, or do they have to stand up in front of the congregation as in forums like "Congregational Appeal" at World Changers Church International!

I believe many congregants deliberately suffer to allow themselves privacy, therefore not to interject their situations into their ministries. Many are doing this, feeling their assemblies aren't confidential, not desiring to entrust their personal/financial information to others! Congregants retain the right to their personal choices regarding how they choose to entrust information but must use wisdom regarding the urgency of many needs.

Congregants should begin using alternative sources when determining if ministries can't assist them. This is one reason why congregants cannot begin affording all the aspects of their ministries every time the man or woman of God is calling the House in a particular direction. Begin saving money, as many times unforeseen circumstances can be taken care of when individuals have some kinds of savings. Prepare in advance for situations that may place debt or inconveniences on yourself and your family, as your assembly may or may not be your first option when in need.

It's sad that we have to discuss these changes now affecting our sanctuaries! I don't believe this situation will soon become better as the days could progress whereas our assemblies will not be able to supply any refuge if there were ever a major emergency affecting a large group of people! Many look to our assemblies as the place of refuge when there is a need, but we must self-prepare, as this may not always be the case. I guess if you're a leader or notable family of an assembly, then resources of some kind may be extended, but in the event of a real emergency, congregants shouldn't be segregated by their non-attachment to leadership or auxiliaries of the church!

As you begin investigating the strategies of your ministry, make sure you understand that the ministry should have a plan or program in place (non-segregated) that is structured to help in all situations! If this program/source doesn't exist, make sure the ministry isn't outsourcing funding, claiming to serve those outside of the ministry while disregarding congregants that support internally. It's going to take diligence, having knowledgeable individuals to implement programs and sources that will effectively meet the needs of congregants as; Christ becomes broken hearted observing how His sheep has no support, as the wolves feast and rest comfortably! When assemblies begin implementing programs and sources, congregants who support the ministry should be the priority!

3.4 Mentors
(Spiritual Fathers and Role Models)

The scope of ministry is always targeted for increase, so we must keep in mind there are those that watch to compete and of course those whom document progression! Pastor leadership conferences are beginning to make their way to the front line, as many are seeking to establish increasing ministries. Some say that these large and sometimes expensive conferences are excellent for pastors, deacons and their wives, ministry leaders, educational ministers, ministers' wives and their children, musicians, drama leaders, youth and preschoolers, recreation administrators, church secretaries and other staffing, even congregants!

Many question how some doctrines are able to impact a large number of congregations so quickly. Well, in these types of forums doctrines, teachings, and other practices are demonstrated to our leaders. Although the walls of denomination, including ethic backgrounds unfortunately segregates ministries, the structure is still open to infiltrate a doctrine for our leaders! The danger of these conferences often seems to impact new pastors, who are trying to escalate congregational growth or other areas of ministry too quickly! Many don't understand that it has taken pastors decades to groom their assemblies to the levels in which they operate, although in today's society, many are boasting of expanding growth in less than five years.

It's imperative for new ministry leaders to understand that what worked for Elder EDF may or may not work for Evangelist OPQ! Some believe the design of ministry wasn't established to meet everyone on the same level, even providing for people at the same time! Therefore, early pastors cannot assume many strategies will work for their congregations! Many early pastors are known to struggle with their congregants as they try to implement strategies learned from either watching television or by attending a specific conference. Congregants, typically hesitate when there appears to be something unusual during worship, as it's common for us not to comply until we're peaceful regarding direction! Year after year, pastors seek to study the latest trends available to the Church community, as this places caution on the hearts of many congregants.

Congregants would be surprised when attending a leadership conference to see the disorder among our leaders. Our leaders tend to beat us up regarding our behavior, but there is no authority available to discipline leaders when necessary. When our leaders are out of control, many times congregants have no say because there is no other authority to report to. Therefore, it's becoming increasingly common that our leaders are growing more and more out of control, having no accountability or authority to sanction occurrences.

When congregants begin researching how many men and women of God are ordained, licensed, certified, or assigned into leadership capacities, you should understand there to be a major problem within the structure. Unfortunately, the walls of denomination, including segregated ministries under a non-denominational umbrella, choose to retain authority in regards to conducting ordination. This practice will continually cause or bring speculation as to how individuals are supposedly representing their titles. As there doesn't appear to be any organization across the realms of Christianity that could valid or verify credentials, congregants will continually become victims, and there will increasingly be individuals trying to form churches in our communities.

When individuals desire to verify credentials of a physician, attorney, or other type of skilled professional, they are able to contact a certification board, agency, or organization to obtain public information. This source doesn't exist in ministry across Christianity. Congregants are only able to inquire regarding the former church from where a ministry leader has come. Many pastors don't specifically take the time to verify ministers that seek to attach themselves to a particular ministry, as many are becoming lazy and disregarding the verification process within the same denomination.

We are in great need of an organization consisting of many divisions serving in the best interests of congregants across Christianity. With the advent of The Ministry Bureau (read Section 6.2) in the next few years, we will definitely see tremendous progress toward setting order across the Body of Christ. It is extremely important that we begin understanding there to be a major problem that has been in operation for long periods of time, hurting and turning individuals against churches, pastors and ministries, which no-one really seems to care. The only time we feel

THE PRICE TAG

some kind of responsibility is when our feelings get hurt or when we're offended. Begin to document your behavior when these kinds of occurrences take place, and you'll see how thousands, even millions have reacted as well.

As pastors and ministry leaders will continue to ordain, license, and certify hundreds of individuals, we must be prayerful that the authority uses wisdom in sending individuals out to serve. Although it's challenging at times to understand the hearts of those who serve, there must be a continual communication channel so ministers are prepared to adapt to the coming changes in ministry. For years pastors have been able to conduct and operate with freewill regarding how they structure their assemblies, but this will soon change, as there are going to become standards for operation. Congregants will be able to know instantly if a ministry is in compliance.

This is going to be a lot of hard work in the coming years, as congregants cannot sit back waiting for a miracle—another problem we face in the body of Christ. It's going to take all congregants within every assembly making sure they understand the compliance in which ministries must operate, including how we must educate ourselves to help our assemblies meet their requirements. This must be a joint effort, as pastors must be adamant regarding strengthening their leaders. Many ministry leaders don't comply with the same visions of their pastors, earnestly desiring to detach themselves, pursuing their own things. Pastors should clearly understand the blueprints of their ministers, as they'll find that many conflict with the ministry's direction and vision.

Increasingly, pastors are requiring ministers who serve under them to establish branches and subsidiaries within the same ministry. This has been favorable for many early pastors, as there are those who still seek to establish their own assembly.

These kinds of situations place speculation of why many ministers desire to serve under a specific ministry. Most congregants are not aware of how their ministries operate, for if there were an opportunity to become knowledgeable of ministry formation, including leadership assignment, many of them wouldn't attend the assembly of choice.

Mentors, spiritual fathers and leaders has always seemed to have been a way for early pastors to begin strengthening their wings, as some still seek to fly on their own. There has always been the statement of how *God has called some and then there are those that have went on their own.* Surprisingly, many have problems submitting to authority, as they continually seek for their congregants to submit to their authority. It's surprising that many pastors and ministry leaders aren't as disciplined as you would think. When ministry leaders are placed in a reversed setting becoming a congregant, you'll be surprised to see how things instantly changes; as many have problems functioning when not behind the pulpit.

Leadership conferences should assist pastors and ministry leaders in strengthening and adapting to all the things they advise us as congregants to accomplish. I believe it necessary for pastors and ministry leaders, twice a year, getting involved in some area of ministry where they're not leading, but following the instructions of others. This should be a reminder for all leaders to evaluate submitting to authority. When our leaders are out of control, what can you expect of the body? When our leaders are speaking the wrong things, how are you expecting congregants to declare the Word effectively? When our leaders are observed deliberating rules and regulations and doing the very opposite, what are you going to expect of congregants? When a large percentage of congregants are heading in wrong directions, don't be quick to verbally abuse them, but check what's been happening in the leadership.

Our leaders understand that as congregants we sometimes rebel against what's right and holy, but there shouldn't be any further influence from our leaders. Many times we're purposely pursuing the wrong, already angry by choice. Parents are able to recognize this kind of behavior with their children, and ministry leaders should be able to recognize the same from their congregants. We as God-chosen people are delicate individuals that obtain the same power as our leaders. Leadership shouldn't victimize us at any time, as it places leadership in jeopardy. How are assemblies going to operate or pursue the work of the Kingdom if God's people are internally wounded, insecure, and constantly troubled regarding their authority/position in Christ Jesus? It's a horrible illustration to observe occurrences inflicted by our own leaders.

If leaders truly desire to become mentors, there shouldn't be any overdubbing of the Word. Leaders must not infiltrate their segregated and biased doctrines into what the Word has to say regarding the authority of leaders. Many who have chosen to mentor in the past and the present have sent out wolves to torture the sheep, delivering back to the House triumphantly, but clearly having wool coats, wool hats, wool pocketbooks, and of course, wool shoes. This behavior has caused thousands, possibly millions, to stray from the Church. Leaving God's people out in the cold, while the House continues to feast and celebrate the goodness of the Lord. The celebration and goodness only begins when those lost sheep have returned back to the House. So, turn off your music, turn your dimmed lights back up, place your finest silverware and ordainments away, and head out of the House with your searchlights on full beams. Then, after the lost has returned, that is the signal to start celebrating.

CHAPTER FOUR

MASS MEDIA EVANGELISM

4.1 Paid Programming
(Televangelism and Radio Ministry)

Some choose to swim the shallow, while others strive to pursue the deep. Today's electronic/mass media integration has facilitated an increasingly progressive system within thousands of ministries, domestic and internationally. Congregants and other viewers can comfortably tune into Christian television networks or other stations to experience televangelism. Televangelism is a unique realm, compared to sanctuary worship services, as its financials many times are transactional-based versus freewill offering. The premise clearly appears as a televised version of what typically happens during a particular worship service held within a local assembly, but the premise can be produced much differently. Televangelism, in my opinion, sometimes offers viewers a compromised version of what a ministry extends to an actual congregant. As mentioned before, I call it the cut-and-paste method, as ministries will consolidate and edit many good

THE PRICE TAG

segments of a particular teaching, thereby confusing viewers, who cannot determine the effective leverage of the teaching.

While the stability of our sanctuary worship services are maintained by our tithes and offerings, including the funding from identified and unidentified sources paid programming uses other strategic methods to survive. The forum of televangelism has proven deep waters for many ministries desiring to syndicate programming, as radio many times is a starting point before pursuing television. Many ministries are affording their paid programming expenses through the assembly's primary cost center/church operation, while others have chosen to separate their syndication expenses, by forming an additional organization/ministry.

If you decide to tune into religious programming, whether televised or on the radio, you can become confused, obtaining mixed understanding of biblical principals and doctrines. Increasingly, it's becoming a big circus when watching back-to-back episodes of many pastors and ministry leaders, as the forum is becoming more competitive and definitely manipulative. As congregants are now beginning to raise many concerns regarding manipulation in their local assemblies, viewers and listeners have always been able to experience manipulation in the comforts of their own homes, as they obtain the same teaching and study habits offered in their local assemblies. But they're still not able to use wisdom when determining how to deal with ministry leaders' solicitations at the end of programs, as many feel overwhelmed when trying to enjoy religious content on the air.

Television and radio evangelists use the forum to solicit seed offerings, vows, pledges, and even tithes (read Section 4.3) to assist with the continual broadcasting efforts of the ministry. It sometimes becomes hilarious when leaders look into the camera lenses, as if they're directly talking to us regarding giving to their ministry. Many are indeed rehearsed, using dramatic, enticing tactics, luring our sentiment and sympathy.

How are congregants and viewers able to afford/support all of the ministries that are now on our televisions and radios? Should we feel guilty not supporting these broadcasts? Why are we ambushed with so much solicitation even during one episode? Week after week, episode after episode, ministry leaders are trying to compel our continual support as if they're the only ones doing a specific work for the Kingdom of God. It's bad enough that congregants are now experiencing this behavior while sitting in our sanctuaries week after week, but now when we turn on our televisions and radios, we're ambushed with the same practices. Increasingly, viewers and listeners focus to enjoy the program, and then proceed to turn the channel/dial right before the solicitation begins.

Many congregants and viewers don't understand how paid programming differs from what we're accustomed to watching on other channels. When we're watching other networks, the commercials that appear every eight to twelve minutes pay for the time to run the program. Sponsors purchase commercial time with television networks, syndication distributors, and even production companies to air commercials within their programs. This gives a sponsor opportunity to reach the targeted demographics for each program.

Paid programming operates in a different forum, as sponsors don't purchase commercial time within syndicated programs. Therefore, the entity that chooses to syndicate, must use a brokerage firm or simply contact each station directly, seeking availability of timeslots designated for paid programming. Entities that seek these timeslots are contracted under terms requiring pay to a network/affiliate or an independent station for the requested time. This entity must maintain its commitment with the network/affiliate or independent station, because there are always others trying to purchase the same timeslot. Therefore, ministries must solicit on a continual basis to maintain their position.

I know I didn't designate a chapter or section of this book to give you information regarding the formation processes of a ministry, but I'll quickly give you some information regarding a church or ministry's tax-exempt business formation. Obtaining a tax-exempt status from the IRS (Internal Revenue Service), business owners who elect to form a non-profit organization or ministry are governed by limitation in regards to their earning capacity. The IRS stipulates several categories in which business owners seeking to obtain a tax-exempt status must state their *General Nature of Activity*. When organizations/businesses choose to form a church/ministry, it is common for business owners to elect the IRC (Internal Revenue Code) Section 501(c) (3)—*public charity or private foundations established for purposes that are religious, educational, charitable, scientific, literary, testing for public safety, fostering of national or international amateur sports, or prevention of cruelty to animals and children*. This category sets forth the structure in which the IRS will approve an organization having a tax-exempt status.

Your assembly may be known by its specific name, but what happens when your ministry leader chooses to use his or her name as a separate entity for business? This is done simply to separate the category *General Nature of Activity* in which he or she is electing to operate or do business. Many times, our leaders are the worst copycats on the planet, as they mingle amongst each other, studying and discovering ways to increase profit margins for their assemblies, including additional personal income for themselves if they have formed or established their own church.

As mentioned previously, if your pastor was hired to conduct pastoral obligation for a particular assembly, he or she is placed on salary or compensated by the assembly through contributions and funding. When a pastor forms or establishes his/her own ministry, he/she retains the right to determine his/her own salary, which must be reported to the IRS, and all of its expenses for operation. Income in addition to stated expenses would be tax exempt (Section 501(c) (3)) and carried over to the next fiscal year for operation. It is illegal for pastors and ministry leaders to live right out of the offering baskets, having unincorporated ministries, obtaining contributions and donations to operate. If a pastor or ministry leader has not incorporated his or her own ministry, including obtaining a tax-exempt status from the IRS, he/she should begin keeping accurate records of contributions, specifying the total amounts received as additional income on his/her personal yearly income taxes.

For example, ABC Church of God may decide to operate their syndication efforts as Bishop XYZ Ministries for broadcasting, separating income, cost centers, and budgets of the ministry. When leaders decide to elect a separate category *General Nature of Activity*, most times its purpose is to specify separate income generated from product sales for leaders. So at the end of the program, when Bishop XYZ Ministries begins to solicit product offers and/or events, this then becomes separate income for Bishop XYZ Ministries, instead of ABC Church of God in which he may be pastor. I hope you understand what I'm trying to relay here. Not all of our leaders are pulling money out of the church/assembly, affording luxurious lifestyles. Many seek to develop products and evangelize frequently, with hopes of earning extra income in addition to what is being paid through the ministry. Did you get that? Ministry leaders wouldn't want to bankrupt their assemblies

THE PRICE TAG

trying to afford the deep expenses of syndicated television and radio programming. In the former years of television and radio, ministry leaders were eager to get into the vast margin potentials of household viewers and listeners, but now with expanded cable and satellite alternatives, even the World Wide Web, leaders have gained more accessibility, seeking to expand and initiate their ministries into syndication markets.

The syndication procedure for paid programming is a pricy business, but can deliver unbelievable profits. As sanctuary income is limited regarding the capacity of regularly attending congregants, television and radio allow ministries to reach into profit potentials of those that don't necessarily attend church. Many individuals don't attend a local assembly but enjoy the comforts of Christian programming via television or radio. Ministry leaders have found this rewarding, as religious programming is increasingly changing its structure. A typical thirty-minute program strip seemed adequate to reach a viewer or listener, but now commercials are making their way into the program content, initiated by leaders, and taking away from teaching the Word. It is often annoying to watch or listen to these programs, as when you're earnestly trying to understand the teaching, you're then interrupted by a commercial solicitation by the ministry. It's almost the same experience as sitting in a congregation, trying to focus on the teaching, when someone feels the need to squeeze out of the row, making his or her way to the aisle.

Viewers and listeners have grown accustomed to traditional paid programming ventures such as skin care solutions, diet and/or food systems, exercise equipment, and even the latest kitchen and household domestic tools. But now ministries are adapting identical solicitation efforts before the close of its programs. Nearly eighty percent of all ministries solicit to support the expenses of their programs, as today there is a declining effort for quality programming (in the USA), as there are now nearly two hours of paid programming (majority ministries), whereas viewers/listeners now have to decide what programs/ministries they're going to watch/afford. Competition has now confused the average viewer/listener whereas, many are now choosing a program as if when watching their favorite sitcom. *All of them are going to ask for something, but you can't afford to give everybody.* With expanding opportunities for ministries seeking to syndicate programming, viewers and listeners are becoming even more frustrated, feeling they're now paying for the Word!

Televangelism is one of fastest forums in which ministry leaders can observe many practices and doctrines, with motives for implementation into their own assemblies. Many times congregants are able to pick up on certain practices by watching what others are doing. This doesn't validate that God approves the practice, but congregants are still easily influenced, when watching others comply with sanctuary movements. Our leaders don't necessarily have to study or seek God for direction for their assemblies, as many are simply watching other leaders on television, speaking the same things to their assemblies. It's discouraging when congregants choose to fellowship with other ministries, discovering identical visions and practices.

Why would a ministry desire to seek deep waters for paid programming? What is the motive behind why our leaders strive to pursue this very expensive forum, which many cannot afford? When observing the number of ministries syndicating programming, many have the same message. Of course the message is always evangelically based, but how can you compete when you're distributing the same message? I know you're asking yourself, why would a ministry choose to compete, as it all should be used for Kingdom building and

THE PRICE TAG

nothing else. Well, I must tell you, that television and radio are as competitive as your favorite sport. Programming directors are watching their ratings as when analyzing them with other programs. This helps to determine profit potentials for timeslots offered by the station for paid programming. Therefore, ministries must make sure viewers and listeners are tuned into the program. When ratings fall, you may tune in the next day to find another ministry in its place.

Paid programming costs can ranges from several hundreds of thousands of dollars per month and even soaring up into the millions. The more markets and stations, the more outsourced monies from the ministry. You may have noticed how ministries are now over-syndicating programs. In other words, you may watch Bishop XYZ Ministries on your cable or satellite station, and then afterwards, turn to your local television station to see the same episode. Many are striving to occupy too many stations, which equates to thousands of more dollars outsourced from the ministry. Guess who has to pay for these kinds of things? That's right: congregants, partners, viewers, and listeners of these programs. They will always ask us to support their stability.

I must use the following example again to demonstrate how ministries cannot afford this forum. In the summer of 2004, Dr. Creflo A. Dollar Ministries syndicating the Changing Your World broadcast had experienced a few millions in debt, as they were not able to afford their market/station distribution scope. The ministry solicited the entire nation and world to help the broadcast, asking for thirty-five dollars from each viewer. So I'm asking again, what will begin happening when every ministry feels the need to solicit, asking us to clear up millions of dollars of debt? How are we going to be able to afford to do this? I personally believe many ministries are on too many channels, competing to boast of their distribution map. The top programs we all know (I won't mention any names) pay out between twenty to forty million dollars a year. Do you want me to say that again? Oh, yes, brothers and sisters, many of the top programs actually pay out two to five millions dollars a month, which soars up into eight-digit budgets annually.

Why are ministries paying out that much money? Is it really for Kingdom building or is there another motive of payoff? We live in a compulsive society; it always spells out more and more and faster and faster. What many of us are not thinking about is the effect this has on those that need to save money for the stability of their own families. Am I saying we should rid ministries of this type of syndication? No! Religious programming is a useful forum, as millions are blessed by it daily, but we're not forecasting three to five years from now, as congregants, viewers, and listeners will begin to experience hardship, supporting the debt of too many ministries!

How many ministries are you supporting financially, whether it's your local assembly or others? How can the average congregant support his or her own assembly, while supporting many outreach ministries and forums? Most times, we're not even aware of what we're doing, as our mentality has changed regarding our behavior. Many congregants still retain the belief to purchase their way into God's presence by continuing to transact upon what feels good and sounds right to the ears, yet they have no confirmation in the heart. It's okay to purchase product offers that can further your study or knowledge regarding a specific biblical topic. But many have lined their bookshelves and libraries with hundreds of items, while they still cannot love their neighbor, even themselves.

After you've purchased all the commodities you believe are assets to your spiritual walk with God, you should be able to pass your understanding on to someone else that may need it. What congregants are experiencing while watching and listening to segments from television and radio may not be the same experience when you receive your package in the mail. Don't allow your emotions from watching television entice you to grab your wallet or purse, reaching for the phone. Television has an alluring presence, which can get you pumped up and heading in the wrong direction. Marketing and promotion campaigns are used exactly for this purpose. Begin seeking God for His direction as it relates to how you are spending your money. Just because it's Bishop XYZ doesn't mean you have to buy what he's offering. Just because Bishop XYZ makes you feel good doesn't mean you have to support everything he targets. If this becomes your behavior, maybe you should begin asking yourself, "Am I a fan of Bishop XYZ, or am I a supporter of the Gospel?"

With millions paid out annually toward syndication efforts of ministries, I wonder how much of those budgets are used to pay individuals for their services rendered to the ministry? How much of the mentioned budget is used to better the community of the ministry (non-segregated)? How much of these budgets can be used to supply refuge for congregants? I know these ministries are most times a separate entity from the actual assembly, but there could still be some allocation for congregants. This behavior can dampen the entire focus of what we call ministry, as when you begin examining the premise, you'll definitely find corruption in many areas.

Continuing to gain understanding, regarding the structure of paid programming, we as believers must wake up now and begin to clearly understand what we believe we're doing in hopes of blessing, versus what we're doing in hopes of blessing a ministry. Most of the time our focus is in the wrong place because we don't have the right information. Ministries will always tell you exactly what you want to hear, because it's the same strategy used in sales to control the way consumers think about obtaining commodities. We're messed up in our thinking, and our society is too compulsive. We have to renew how we empower our thoughts about spending money, as we're headed in the wrong direction when we believe religious commodities bring us closer to God.

4.2 eMinistry and Virtual Pastors

From radio to television, with cassettes tapes and now DVDs, the motive to spread the Gospel of Jesus Christ doesn't seem difficult. As our ministry leaders continue to integrate technology into their ministries, congregants will begin to see more enhancements, which will become luxuries for some and a waste of money to others. Technology in several eyes can become costly when factoring implementation into a ministry. I'm not referring to information technology (IT) structures used to operate a ministry's enhanced technology; I'm talking about how congregants are able to utilize technology alternatives within their assemblies.

Many ministries are moving in the direction of supplying congregants with Ethernet and wireless alternatives for laptop users during church services. Some are even incorporating cell phone blockers (preventing your cell phone from getting a signal) into their assemblies, as several hotels have done. The latest technology will always be a pamphlet and a consultant/technician away. Can our ministries keep up with the latest and greatest at the expense of congregants?

Not only have ministries begun incorporating technology solutions into their assemblies, but many are also investing big dollars for outreach. Due to the overwhelming number of ministries now desiring to syndicate programming on television and radio, many are now heading toward the World Wide Web. From streaming to progressive video segments offered as live broadcasts or playbacks, ministries are utilizing all alternatives to spread the Gospel. As encouraging as these alternatives are becoming, many ministries aren't prepared to handle the servicing and maintenance to operate in these capacities.

Believers are becoming spoiled with many of these alternatives, as there are positive and negative outcomes from these choices. Congregants, which develop study habits that feed from outreach ministries that broadcast, have found the electronic forum very useful for obtaining information quicker. These forums have also become a tool for congregants to view a broad spectrum of the latest happenings in the Christian community. From news to entertainment and your basic outreach servicing for ministry, believers and viewers are able to access the world from the comfort of their homes or any place where we can access the Web.

Although, these alternatives have become luxuries, supplying believers with choices better governing their time and even money, congregants are utilizing these alternatives without using wisdom. Believers have begun withdrawing their attendance from their local assemblies because they now have the ability to watch their own ministry on the Web. While many ministry leaders advise their congregants that the alternative is actually targeted for those who are unable to attend church due to sickness, work schedules, etc., many congregants have adapted this alternative for lazy behavior.

As more and more congregants are utilizing this alternative and not attending church, leaders are noticing a decline in attendance, especially within Tithes and Offering margins. The odds of the individuals giving offering or returning tithes are very slim, because congregants choose to stay home to listen or view broadcast services on the Web, television, or on the radio. Leaders are becoming aware that these alternatives have positive and negative outcomes and now want to govern how congregants are utilizing these sources.

With a decline in financial support from congregants choosing to stay at home, being reluctant giving offering and returning tithes, this creates a motive for leaders seeking to intercept what other pastors are not receiving monetarily. Virtual pastors are stepping on the scene, as now electronic ministries are making their way onto the Web. A digital camera, a streaming video provider, marketing allocations, a post office box in several regional areas of the world can get a preacher on the Web much faster than trying to form a local assembly. Many believe this new wave of ministry is going to become the latest trend. By then preachers will able to set up shop right in the comfort of their homes, pressing buttons and positioning the camera right from a chair, having limited overhead and, of course, obtaining substantial profits.

We have to begin forecasting the progression of ministries now desiring to embrace alternatives that will always be documented as *spreading the Gospel around the world*. If millions of people are sending millions of dollars each month through the mail supporting televangelists, imagine how many will be adapting an identical flow for eMinistries having virtual pastors. The first question that comes to my mind is, "Who's going to pay for ministries trying to execute their scope of work?" The answer is the same individuals that have been paying for decades.

I was watching a female evangelist based in Florida, who is now becoming popular in the Christian community on television. I began observing how she was adapting to the common strategies to solicit support of her broadcasting endeavors. This female evangelist was building a television studio, so she'll be able to broadcast her syndication endeavors from a soundstage instead of a

THE PRICE TAG

sanctuary. She began soliciting the world to support the purchase of all of her broadcasting equipment and integration. This pricy million-dollar invoice was used to solicit viewers to afford her evangelism platform. Twenty-five to thirty or more ministries broadcast regularly on a particular network. How are we going to be able to afford the broadcast equipment, including integration of many of them, as technology will change and become outdated?

These situation may not affect your finances right now, but wait until the world of technology introduces the next latest and greatest, which ministry leaders will desire to integrate into their ministries. Congregants, viewers, and listeners will be solicited to begin supporting these alternatives. This is what's happening now with eMinistries and virtual pastors. I understand that is does cost money to operate anything, but the question must be what can I afford, what should I afford, and what is not wise to afford? There are too many leaders mentioning they're trying to reach the world with the Gospel, but they cannot afford to do so. I'm still confused as to who is going to support the stability of many of these ministries.

Of course, many of us have tuned into one of these kinds of ministries, and it makes us feel guilty when they're asking for support and we choose not to give. The average believer can't support every broadcast or stream of video that he or she watches or listens to. If this were factual, many believers wouldn't utilize these alternatives knowing there to be a price tag attached. We know these alternatives are useful, having a positive impact, as they are a needed source for those who are unable to receive many luxuries of the Gospel that we enjoy. So, how can we stipulate what we can afford and what we cannot? Internet, television, and radio are becoming additional extensions to what many ministries are contributing to their expanding budgets for outreach.

Do you believe assemblies should begin incorporating technological luxuries without the consent of congregants having to support this alternative? Should believers independently have to continue being solicited by the increasing number of eMinistries and virtual pastors? Should viewers and listeners begin funding the expense of ministries desiring to purchase broadcast equipment for outreach purposes? Do you believe congregants will begin to feel bad if ministries can no longer afford their progressive endeavors, ending their broadcasts?

Having an impact to deliver awareness regarding how believers spend their money, including how we contribute supporting outreach, these questions are all relevant. Until congregants begin understanding the expense structures of ministry, including their obligation and freewill option, many will become victims to unforeseen changes making their way to the forefront. Our decisions and opinions are continually targeted for manipulation; it's our responsibility to educate ourselves of these recent changes. Television broadcasting, including cable and satellite alternatives, has limitations regarding the number of stations available to viewers, but the World Wide Web contains no parameters; therefore, leaders will not have difficulty launching a ministry, or becoming a Virtual pastor with no association to a physical assembly.

Can you imagine the number of Web sites that will begin to make their way into the households of millions? E-commerce alternatives will most likely incorporate their way into the same structure, as that is how ministries solicit us to purchase product offers. No longer will congregants have to get dressed, preparing themselves for a worship experience within a corporate environment for praise and worship, as eMinistries will either broadcast live or pre-recorded services as an alternative for believers. This spells out more campaigns, direct mail solicitation, and increasing telemarketing. These requests will definitely outline beautiful brochures expressing the objective for outreach mentioning signature Scriptures and quotations used for sympathy and compassion. Still outlining partnering support, monthly/weekly contributions, soliciting your tithes and even referrals. This is the direction in which we're going as a Christian community stating that we're trying to reach the world with the Gospel!

What are your feelings regarding ministries selling database information to other ministries, desiring to market their product offers and services? Where else would a new ministry or entity obtain names of thousands, possibly millions of potential customers even those whom have purchased product in the past? Ministries may use their database information as a way of producing additional income and will supply such information as our names, mailing addresses, and telephone numbers to entities around the world. It's becoming common for ministries to document our employers, pay schedules, number of children, and other personal aspects of our lives. To make sure information is documented accurately; ministries may begin asking for our social security numbers, which may lead into obtaining credit information verifying our identities. At this time, this may appear unbelievable, but as our society is moving progressively toward taking away the opinions and decisions of people, we should expect more businesses, including ministries, to do the same.

How many times have you filled out one form and then had your contact information shared among other companies who sent you solicitation? This kind of transaction can happen very quickly. If you're not the type of person who places your personal information in many places, you'll probably be able to pinpoint the source that has shared your information. Please begin understanding the number of ministries with your personal information and observe the potentials of that information being sold or viewed by others.

Can you imagine driving into your church's parking lot, being handed a voice box to place in your vehicle since the sanctuary and overflow rooms are full? Can you image being advised that your church's services are now offered via pay-per-view? Imagine your local assembly charging a per-person charge for admission? The day will come when ministries will begin requiring a username and password to access their computer servers and hear the Word of God. If we don't get a handle on situations now affecting the Christian community, these aspects and others will increasingly become part of how believers choose to worship!

Not forsaking the assembling of ourselves together, as the manner of some is; but exhorting one another: and so much the more, as ye see the day approaching (Hebrews 10:25). Are eMinistries and virtual pastors God's design for those that still choose to forsake the assembling? Are congregants choosing to stay home, as there are many situations now affecting their decisions? Typically, we as the Church tend to judge individuals when discovering that a congregant may choose not to attend a local assembly. We don't have anything deep or spiritual to say; therefore, we either quickly toss Hebrews 10:25 at the individual (oh, we're good for tossing scripture), or we try our best to encourage the person to at least attend another assembly.

Religion, primary the history of Christianity, has broken off into many areas, which has established several denominations and doctrines, creating variety. Therefore, believers retain a choice of how and where they choose to worship, making finding a good church home one of the most challenging things on earth. Preference seems to be our first priority when making a choice of

THE PRICE TAG

where and how we desire to worship. We have several choices these days, choosing between doctrines and techniques. We retain preference observing demographics of the House, by analyzing age mean, families with children verses, too many singles with too many children, too many women having limited to no active men in the ministry and etc... Many congregants factor music ministry, including the variety of sanctuary auxiliaries extended, making sure the House doesn't become boring having a traditional structure that doesn't change even within a ten-year bracket. Location and accessibility are important to many congregants' even reputation and notability.

You may believe these changes are too personalized, but due to the way we retain preference, this encourages congregants to analyze several areas before deciding where and how to worship. Some believe these choices are too complicated and many then settle for television, radio, or Internet ministries. Having these options, many can situate themselves as if watching their favorite program on television. As the comforts of individuals' homes are becoming more desirable, many ministry leaders are concerned with how it will affect their profit margins. Many feel church has changed its structure, becoming more business-oriented rather than representing the cross of Calvary. Although, many still don't follow or accept the message of salvation, there are still those who believe on the name of the Lord and attend church, encouraged to hear the message. Changes have flushed out the message, implementing a convergence of economics, which only benefits the House and those in authority, leaving congregants and other ministry supporters broke and hurting. This will definitely make the new wave of eMinistries and virtual pastors a priority, as many will continue to seek comforting for the broken areas of our lives.

4.3 The Fight for the Tithe

Why are outreach ministries and other types of ministries now soliciting congregants to return tithes into their organizations? The Bible tells us in (Malachi 3:10) *Bring ye all the tithes into the storehouse...* How we conduct ministry has become a broad spectrum, as many ministry leaders are now requesting the tithe to be returned to the place where the individual is general obtaining the Word. Due to compromising situations affecting our sanctuaries, many believers are now rethinking how they're obtaining the Word, and many have settled for televangelism and radio ministries. Congregants have begun limiting their attendance now that there are an increasing number of ministries on the air.

The broadcast industry of television and radio is still a competitive forum; therefore, ministry leaders are restructuring how viewers and listeners can give. As many ventures observed have proven successful, congregants should know there are always others in the works, which they may or may not be prepared for. Controversy continues to rise as congregants, viewers, and listeners are now being told where we should return our tithes. Many leaders, primarily in television, are now stipulating that viewers should return their tithes to their broadcast ministry! Leaders have clearly been observed soliciting viewers who watch their program on a regular basis, to return tithes into their ministry/assemblies. Ministries are justifying this solicitation by stating, *viewers should return the tithe to the place where they're obtaining the Word.*

Increasingly, televised religious programs have become more convenient since you don't have to leave the comfort of your home to attend church, but this doctrine now has caused local assemblies (non-broadcasting) to become stern with their members, regarding

THE PRICE TAG

the interruption of finances being contributed into the House. *Now they're fighting over the tithes; Help us Lord!* Congregants have begun subtracting their financial contributions, including their tithes, submitting them to broadcasting ministries. This is a serious situation, as local assemblies are beginning to see a decrease in their tithes and offering margins.

Not only are broadcasting ministries soliciting you to return your tithes to their particular ministry, but I've personal observed TBN (Trinity Broadcasting Network) stating that you can send your tithes to them too. Of course you have to tune into a specific television network to watch a particular program, so how is it that now, networks, including the programs in which it airs are soliciting viewers for tithes? If you don't know by now, we are in serious trouble, as I've personally witnessed someone subtracting her tithes from her local assembly, contributing them to a broadcasted ministry on television. This was evidence that viewers are being solicited, and some believe this practice to be justified.

I must say this subject appears situational, as there was a time when I didn't have a local assembly in which I was a member. Therefore, I would return my tithes to the ministry in which I fellowshipped. Although I wasn't a member, when the ministry leader would call for tithers, I returned them accordingly. I believe many congregants find themselves in similar situations, not being a member of a particular assembly, but desiring to return the tithe. This can create or intrigue the motives of pastors and ministry leaders, as many desire to obtain tithes of other congregants as well. Some believers choose to withhold tithes when not a member of a particular assembly, as many believe they will continue to be led by the Spirit, where and even when, to return tithes having specific instruction.

Should there be a centralized place for congregants to return their tithes if they're not a member of a particular assembly? Should congregants continue to return tithes to their former assembly until they've joined another? Should believers continue to be led as to where they should return tithes, as it relates to fellowshipping with other ministries? Should believers return tithes to a television network rather than the program in which it airs? Should broadcast ministries be forbidden to solicit viewers for their tithes, being a conflict of interest with the network? Should networks be forbidden to solicit their viewers for tithes, being a conflict of interest with the programs it offers to viewers?

These are all valid questions, and these situations need much clarification. This specific subject matter is controversial, and many leaders will try to stay away from it, while continuing to solicit our tithes. Our leaders are always ready to utilize biblical justifications tactics, earnestly trying to prove a point. Many times this leads us as congregants into making incorrect decisions when trying to do what is biblically correct. It becomes confusing, when one leader says this is the right way; the next program or leader says you should do it that way; and then your own pastor threatens you taking away your decisions and opinions. During this tug-of-war scenario, congregants typically choose not to return the tithe at all!

Is there meat in the storehouse? This is the real question when analyzing the provisions of the assembly you attend. Our tithes are purposed as provision within the House. Are sources for provision being stored in your assembly? Would your ministry be surviving from offering to offering? Who can access the provision when in need? Are you making sure your ministry is able to have provision or are you a hindrance?

4.4 Partnering
(Direct Mail Solicitation and Telemarketing)

With increasing competition in the genre of paid programming, viewers and listeners are confused as to where and whom to give Tithes and Offerings. Ministry leaders have begun strategically restructuring their solicitation methods, with hopes of increasing contributions for their ministries. With exciting product offers, including ministry giveaways, many are still experiencing challenges supporting their broadcasts. Viewers and listeners feel harassed by ministries, as many obtain your mailing address when you order a product or call a designated prayer line for general inquires made to a ministry. *Once you give to or even call these ministries, they put you on their mailing lists and harass you on a monthly basis.* Ministries are increasingly using our personal information from these kinds of transactions, increasing their scope for further solicitation.

Where are congregants getting the money to support several ministries? Previously, I asked how many ministries you were supporting on a monthly or yearly basis. Ten dollars here, twenty dollars there, one hundred and fifty dollars for registration, including your one hundred dollars supposedly seed offering, is causing mass numbers of congregants to accrue debt.

Ministry leaders have now focused a lot of attention on soliciting individuals to become partners. This practice is similar to other leaders soliciting for financial pledges on a monthly basis. Becoming a partner of a ministry then prompts viewers and listeners to make a decision about giving into other ministries. Partnering with a particular ministry signifies an agreement between the ministry and its congregants and supporters.

This enables a ministry to communicate and solicit directly to its supporters exclusively. The mailing of literature, monthly newsletters, and other direct mail solicitation, including an offering envelope, so that congregants, viewers/listeners feel apart of the ministry.

On March 15, 2005, at 12:18 p.m. Eastern Standard Time (USA), I received a call from (C. Walker) of Dr. Creflo A. Dollar Ministries partner relations department. A message was left on my voice mail at my place of business instead of my home phone number. This message was a general solicitation to become a partner of the ministry. I was first puzzled as to how the ministry obtained my name and work phone number. But it had come to me very quickly, as it was initiated from the thirty-five dollar summer solicitation. Do you see what I've been trying to tell you? Once you give to a ministry, even just one time, they will use your former information for continual solicitation as if that's okay. I found this practice to be personally offensive, although I'm learning how not to become quick to offense. These feelings were triggered as I am right in the middle of writing this book, then to check my voice messages at work to find a ministry soliciting me for money; I think this ministry might have caught me at the wrong time.

Why would this ministry go back through their 2004 contribution records searching for names and phone numbers of those who aren't partners soliciting them to become one? I'd given the initial thirty-five dollars, because a friend mentioned the situation, and I desired to support the ministry. I found this situation to be common among many ministries, I believe Dr. Dollar to be a genuine person, and so I chose to give to his ministry. I don't understand why ministries use your one-time contribution or your information from product offers as a way of establishing a long-term relationship. TD Jakes Ministries and TBN have done the

THE PRICE TAG

same in the past. During the same summer, I also called Marilyn Hickey Ministry's prayer line, on one occasion, and I now receive monthly solicitation from this ministry. Nowadays, we can't even pick up the phone to call a prayer line, order merchandise, or give in support of any particular ministry because they are designed to keep a continual hand in our pockets. If we don't get things in order soon, many ministries are going to begin eliminating their toll-free phone numbers, replacing them with 900 numbers, in which callers will have to pay a toll per minute, which will be justified by us helping support the ministry, sowing by phone! God help our phone bills if we get a long-winded prayer warrior on the line praying for political and governmental concerns, when the initial prayer request was for temperance.

I'm not pinpointing these ministries to say they're the only ones operating in this capacity; as you'll discover, nearly eighty percent of all ministries are doing similar things. How are we going to be able to support our local assembly, giving tithes and offering while many are experiencing harassment, as our local assemblies are now seed offering their congregations, including every other kind of offering they can get from the people. Then supporting several outreach ministries, which solicit our support on a monthly basis.

Becoming a partner or a faithful contributor to a particular outreach ministry in which you may or may not be a member, isn't wise, if you're then subtracting your finances from your local assembly. Pastors of local assemblies are becoming furious as their congregants are now making financial contributions into other ministries. Your primary support should go into your local assembly, while outreach ministries should be secondary. You should not begin subtracting your financial contributions from your local assembly, supporting someone else that is on television, radio, or the Internet. When or if there were ever an emergency, do you believe a televangelist is going to be a phone call away? No! It may be the same with our local pastors as well, but your local assembly is the proper protocol for reaching out for help or assistance when needed. Partners and outside supporters of outreach ministries are only a name and mailing address to the ministry, whereas in your local assembly, at least somebody has seen your face at one time or another and could identify you if a situation arises that required identification. Congregants, what are we doing? The only reasons why many outreach ministries have been able to proceed with these kinds of solicitation campaigns and that's because it works.

Your pastor is probably a more sincere preacher than who's on television; you should give your local assembly the money to help further their ministry's blueprints. I found this to be true while a member of TLC, Bishop McDaniel is a phenomenal man of God, which I feel deserves to be on television or some other scope of expanded ministry. This was one of the reasons why I joined the ministry, as I witnessed the potentials of the House. I planned to support from my capacity in regards to getting behind the vision. But as previously mentioned, there were several particulars of the ministry that I later found I couldn't be part of. What I'm trying to tell you is that there is potential in the man or woman of God that you sit/labor under week after week, so why are you funding someone else on television, radio, or the Internet, subtracting your contributions from your local assembly? When giving diligently into your own local assembly, make sure there is real vision first, watch how your church can expand and do great things in and for the community as well.

As ministries have found partnering and direct mail solicitation to be successful, some individuals are affording multiple ministries now feeling the lifestyle of Christianity is becoming too expensive.

THE PRICE TAG

Even with all the T-shirts, buttons, bookmarks, pens, coffee cups, ministry bags, jam-packed bookshelves, and enormous CD and tape collections, believers are even more depressed, still single, getting divorced, and of course going broke. When does this behavior change? How are we going to be able to determine where we should be contributing our finances? How many other ministries are preparing identical campaigns ready for execution? Imagine the number of early pastors meditating on these types of strategies. When are congregants going to no longer tolerate being out of control, making our own decisions, even though ministries are always prepared to market/promote a seemingly wonderful Kingdom-building plan contingent to our giving?

When seeking to partner with a particular ministry, you will most likely receive a fact sheet, which states the vision of the ministry. These beautifully written letters stipulate the definition for being a partner with the ministry. Partnering is a covenant relationship between people who support one another in the achievement of a common goal. The believer/supporter should be an individual who is committed to the ministry and shares the vision. Partnering is typically designed to help believers fulfill the will of God for their lives (Ephesians 4:16 & I Thessalonians 3:1-3).

Ministries in which desire you to partner will send you a partnering kit, which offers partners subscription opportunities, product offer discounts, and other benefits, separating the partner from other givers. Partnering kits typically specify that there is no specific dollar amount requirement for becoming a partner, whereas many believe the partnering amount could be a tenth of what is paid for tithes. Partnering kits require partners to become active by sowing financially, calling and writing the ministry, and ordering products. Some ministries retain a window in which partners should be active; therefore, non-activity will place a partner into a non-active status. This is used to help partners remain good stewards over that which is for the Lord, but assisting the ministry to save money keeping you on their mailing lists and other benefits offered. What determines non-activity for a partner? Well, that shouldn't be a hard question; no financial giving including, no product sales will definitely place a partner in a non-active status. Most likely partner relation departments will begin making phone calls advising their delinquent partners that they have been slipping in their commitment.

Monthly contributions as a partner of a ministry helps leaders travel and evangelize, ministering to the needs of people around the world, possibly where the Gospel is scarce. They also build facilities in certain areas, purchase airtime for their broadcast (if they're a broadcasting ministry), publish and produce materials to help others grow spiritually, conduct outreach mission functions, as well as hosting conventions and the increasing partner-only meetings. The general public typically supports ministries and organizations, which therefore try to offer its partners and supporters first-class services. Just as in any relationship, many should strive not to have a one-sided relationship, mutually exchanging faithfulness toward each other.

Of course, most ministries that conduct direct mail solicitation don't require partnering; whether you give or not, they will continue to solicit in hopes of your support. Ministries are beginning to implement better strategies as there are complaints regarding unsolicited mail received from ministries, and many will continue to keep the solicitation ongoing. Some ministries have several partnering categories; therefore, believers can specify the amount of money they're willing to contribute on a monthly or weekly basis. Categories such as gold, bronze, silver, and even special titles like miracle seed of faith, miracle for multiplication, unusual harvest seed, and proxy seed on special occasions like Easter, Thanksgiving (USA) and Christmas.

Congregants can get caught up so quickly, as ministries will sometimes include symbolic items within their mail solicitation; therefore, individuals feel as if they're getting something every month. As each month comes and goes, congregants, viewers, listeners, and supporters are generating stacks of mail solicitation, including the symbolic giveaways, as many are supporting outside of their capacity into several ministries. Believers may choose to give to a particular ministry, whereas some choose to send money orders within an envelope with no return address to escape the efforts of the ministry placing their personal information within their databases.

Included is a general form letter that I'm advising every congregant, or supporter of ministry to use in order to have their personal information removed from the databases of ministries. It's imperative we begin taking a stand, no longer feeling harassed or voiceless. What ever we tolerate, we cannot change. Therefore, the same things we're taught in our assemblies and by watching religious programming, we must utilize creating a peaceful environment for our lives. Please feel free to use the form letter, making sure it reaches all the ministries from which you want your personal information removed.

By taking a stand, you are now empowering yourself to resume making decisions regarding what you will or will not tolerate. I know many ministries will instantly begin to experience setbacks with a decline in financial contributions, but we must honestly make a choice that we desire to support. As many ministries will begin to close their doors, cancel their broadcasting efforts, or experience other challenges from these coming changes, congregants must remain in position, understanding their rights as believers to be led where and to whom to give.

As compulsive as our society will continue to become, congregants should better understand how to empower themselves retaining their choices. When we choose to support a particular ministry, it should not interfere with our financial commitments to our local assemblies. In addition, our local assemblies shouldn't or continue to stress or manipulate their congregants either, regarding their giving, as congregants should be empowered not supporting the ministry if we choose. These changes may appear harsh or unusual, but when God opens your eyes to the madness that unfolds before congregants day by day and week after week, you'll clearly begin to understand your position and do something about it.

These changes are not only going to better your worship experience in your local assembly, the way you support paid programming, including partnering endeavors, but it's going to spill over into several areas of our lives. You are no longer going to be able to tolerate other types of telemarketing and direct mail solicitation that you receive. Your lifestyle regarding how individuals target to get your attention is going to change. You'll then look back and clearly see how you for so many years have thrown away provision, which could have been used to support the direction in which God is still initially calling you. That's a major problem, when you begin to neglect yourself, pushing aside your own vision, going blind to God's purpose for your life. Then you'll begin feeling prostituted and abused supporting someone else, receiving nothing in return. You won't be able to blame anyone but yourself, as ministries are already prepared to tell you that you lack faith!

Desire to learn and understand more about your local assembly and its direction. Just as you take the time to look for a good school for your children, you should use the same diligence to understand the ministry you attend. Begin asking questions; attend some meetings (don't let them rush you into joining and/or attaching yourself to an auxiliary); try to research the foundation of the ministry regarding former locations, years established, former pastors, current or past scandal; and other information that will empower you to make a sound decision about whether the ministry is for you.

Just because the choir can modulate five times doesn't mean the House is stable. Just because the man or woman of God can modulate the same doesn't mean that is the place where you should worship. It takes time to understand these types of things, and many will try to disregard your empowerment, seeking to control what you think and the things you say. Saying no doesn't make you a bad believer, but empowers you to obtain wisdom and further instruction. That's what we should desire most and that's wisdom, being able to make better decisions regarding how we view and support ministry. If you lack wisdom, just ask God, for He will surely supply you with what you need. With increasing wisdom flowing through the lives of congregants worldwide, we can begin to forecast progression toward the scope of work that is ahead.

D'MOREA JOHNSON

Form Letter (Unsolicited Mail)

Date:
YOUR NAME
Mailing Address
City, State Zip/Postal Code, Country
Re: Unsolicited Mail

Dear (ministry's name),

   Praise the Lord! My name is Brother/Sister (YOUR NAME) your ministry has assigned me the number _____ (it's normally near your name or address, and is used to identify you in their database).

   In an effort to protect my personal information from being fraudulently used and/or unauthorized, I'm writing to have my name, address, telephone, fax number(s), and email address, as well as credit/debit card information and/or other confidential information removed from your database.

   I appreciate your assistance in this matter and hope this letter doesn't in any way appear offensive to your organization/ministry. I understand the efforts you've taken to keep in touch with me regarding your products and services, but at this time; I'm no longer in agreement with many policies initiated by several ministries and organizations.

   I thank you again for understanding my concern(s) and I hope you will have continual success in reaching individuals that can freely accept your solicitation offers. In the future, if I decide to contact your ministry regarding any of your product offers, events, or other areas of service you extend to the public, I will clearly specify what information should be retained for your ministry records. Thank you again for understanding my concern(s) and I appreciate your ministry understanding my request.

Thank You,
Sign your name
Print your name

CHAPTER FIVE

REACHING IN FOR OUTREACH— TAKING OUT FOR PROFIT

5.1 Community Choirs and Recording Groups

Do you know anyone who is currently or formerly a part of a community choir? If so, then you should be well informed of the tremendous amount of dedication involved. I myself, formerly involved in only one community choir in my life have been essential, having been exposed to several areas of ministry, in which the average congregant may not specifically experience within a local assembly. Community choirs are typically made up of several individuals from different churches with denominations of diverse religious backgrounds, but many choirs and groups are predominantly from the same church. It takes a lot of diligence in the foundation process of starting a new choir because leaders typically require a simple verbal and/or signatory membership; in other cases, auditioning is required.

The formation of a community choir creates an environment that is surprisingly different from that of a local assembly because of the common interest. The fellowship of believers that come together having a common interest is a rewarding strength, as the foundation clearly stipulates unity. The collaboration of these kinds of ministries is now structuring their environments, such as with church organizations. Rules and regulations are implemented, and members sometimes take offense, as the forum is generally freewill. Although, members freely choose to become part of community choirs, leaders still structure the environment as if members were part of a church. Instead of taking up offering, leaders many times will request members to pay weekly or monthly dues to fund rehearsal space, fundraising, and other necessities for operation. Some members don't believe they should pay dues; many choirs assign a section leader or other titled individual to keep track of member allocations, as it's common for members to be held responsible for nonpayment.

Weekly rehearsals sometimes become an obligation as leaders try to structure a progressive flow, teaching new songs for development. Leaders try to facilitate the teaching of original songs and music, and some may typically sing material from other recording groups, as it's customary to do both. Leaders' primary focus is to either one day become a recording choir/group or tour to support those who are recording. With this motive, many times members are left out of the business endeavors of the organization because many leaders are only concerned about their names receiving accolades.

Friday and Saturday nights are the typical program circuit forums in which choirs from surrounding areas and sometimes-distant areas come together for concerts, although Sunday afternoon and evening programs are common as well. A typical environment outlines a master of ceremonies to preside over the program, announcing choirs/groups, keeping the program moving. Often, an invited preacher is scheduled to deliver the Word, as many congregants try to tiptoe out the door before he or she gets up to speak. These programs generally attract a distinctive crowd in which you'll begin to become a familiar face after a while.

Conspicuous spectators, fashion police, program saints (those that don't attend regular church-only music programs), fakes dons and divas, the next hottest singers and musicians on the planet, preachers (attending to primarily learn new one-liners) dance-oholics (those that come to dance all night) hot singles ready to mingle (including the married) and the very popular gay and lesbian turn outs. Did I forget anyone? This is the primary crowd who religiously supports these kinds of programs. Many are structured obtaining a freewill offering, as others are sometimes ticketed, if there is a noted recording artist attached to the program. The environments at these programs are more than enough guilty of many of the situations discussed in this book.

The structure of these programs whereas choirs/groups flock to is where individuals generally are exposed to many practices and doctrines not customary within their local assemblies. There remains speculation regarding individuals who for many years have become caught up in the facets of the program circuit, as many backslide after losing enthusiasm, which later progresses to straying away from the Church. There seems to be a cross junction between worship practices in a local assembly to what is found at a program, as local assemblies will most likely stick to a set structure (order of worship) that corporately embraces believers in all walks of life, whereas the program circuit typically attracts individuals having a need to embrace a more charismatic and/or musical experience. Therefore, those who have grown accustomed to the program circuit tend to seek a local assembly that supplies a similar environment. This becomes very tricky, because if a local assembly's structure is that of the program circuit's, there are going to be many situations that other believers may not experience, regarding the environment attracting specific individuals. It has become common that individuals that are accustomed to the program circuit tend to seek pastors that have come from the genre as well.

Pastors who have come from the genre of the program circuit and are later called to pastor don't usually experience the struggles of starting new ministries that those from other environments do. Congregants tend to transition over to these types of ministries, having a stronger connection to their pastors. For some reason, these churches are more progressive and collaborative, having an inclusive environment, coming together for rejoicing, fellowshipping, and fun in the name of the Lord. When traditional congregants come into the mix of these kinds of fellowships, they're spotted, as there is a peculiar difference of those that have come from the program circuit than those whom are more traditionally based. A traditional believer may become sidetracked when there appears to be a slight change in the order of worship, as those whom have been exposed to a more charismatic environment are more abrupt to quickly move with the flow. Being liberated from the traditional "Order of Worship," which many assemblies are aggressive becoming sidetracked; those that have been exposed to the program circuit fully understand how to quickly adapt to the environment.

Pastors many times frown on their members who pursue charismatic environments, as the exposure can place a believer into an unsatisfactory worship setting. When this happens, exposed believers sometimes try to implement additional experiences into their local assembly, which can create problems. Ministry leaders become stern regarding abrupt changes introduced from exposed believers, as many feel they will lose control of other congregants desiring liberation, which will equate to loosing members to other ministries. Although the program circuit exposes believers to a

THE PRICE TAG

seemingly disturbing environment in the eyes of some, it creates the most profound dedication, loyalty, and commitment for tasking. Those who are or were former members of community choirs/groups will tell you of many sacrifices required to get their group off the ground. Many have struggled, creating local and/or regional names for their choirs/groups, and many have financed independent projects and/or events. From choir robes to uniformed apparel, to customizable styles for recognition, members have at all costs invested tremendous amounts of time and money in order to get the name of their choir/group recognized. This heart-driven passion has caused many individuals to become angry, frustrated, and humiliated disregarding their families, careers and other obligations, as many retain suppressed emotions regarding making a name for someone else not receiving anything in return.

Paying for your own transportation, clothing, and admission, as well as selling tickets and merchandise and passing out flyers to promote programs, while participating within a community choir/group oftentimes causes members to feel mistreated, used, neglected, and overlooked. Leaders become adamant regarding getting their names known, overlooking those who have helped for years to get them where they are today. Many times, there are new faces that appear within community choirs/groups due to members being overlooked and disregarded. Members spend months even years appreciating their leaders, traveling from city to city including other endeavors, never being personally appreciated other than being handed some cake and punch after church services.

Depending upon the leverage of a choir/group, sometimes there are ticket prices associated with concerts in which members are not paid for their services rendered, making a substantial profit for their leaders. Although, these budgets are typically used to further the expansion endeavors of the choir/group, it still seems necessary to appreciate those who have helped put money in the bank. Leaders understand there to be a freewill environment associated to these kinds of outreach ministries, as many tend to target the formation, getting individuals together to make money. Many have no desire to give back to those who have helped them, but feel the forum is established for solitary gain. For years, ministries have been able to make tons of money from individuals who commit to a specific task or project; therefore it hasn't become a second thought paying those for their time rendered to their ministries.

Taking a second breath, recording choirs/groups experience identical situations; as members within this caliber retain suppressed emotions feeling mistreated and used as well. Leaders seemed to have forgotten about those who have helped them get to their leveled status, as often you'll always find new faces and increasingly new lead singers. Many recording choirs/groups can't keep a new lead singer from one project to the next. No compensation and no appreciation seem to be the banner, in which members will rise trying to express major concerns. Artists are typically issued a budget toward the production costs of studio and/or live projects. Budgets many times do not include compensation for background singers and choirs that participate in these projects. Leaders, generally pool several singers together and rarely compensate anyone for time rendered.

Having local to regional distribution even national and international sales, record labels do not include background singers and/or choir members within their royalty allocations; payment are generally payable to the leader of the choir/group. Although the project is titled Bishop XYZ and The Voices of LMN, Bishop XYZ will be getting all the money! The Voice of LMN may consist of fifteen singers who supply background vocals, even lead singing on several songs, but are not compensated for their talents used on the

THE PRICE TAG

project generating money. It becomes an offense when Bishop XYZ can't even sing, having his/her name on the project racking up all the money! This is becoming very common in the christian/gospel music recording industry; leaders having a limited amount of vocal ability and/or other production talents are placing their names on recording projects, utilizing real singers, making lots of money!

How is it that leaders can make thousands of dollars utilizing individuals with talent, without compensating those who are the primary cause for generating a sale? Even when recording choirs/groups are on the road in concert (primarily ticketed events), singers are not even compensated for their time. Bishop XYZ may charge each promoter/ministry seventy-five hundred dollars plus transportation to perform in concert and still not compensate members at all. Many will supply meals, lodging, and transportation if applicable, but a large percentage of recording choirs/groups, will not pay their members for their time supporting the ministry.

Many members have lost their jobs, including experienced other situations while traveling on the road. Participating in this genre of outreach, many leaders still have no concern regarding the outcome of member commitments. When members decide to calculate the amount of time and money invested to create a name for someone else, it becomes depressing analyzing the potential value if they were involved in something more constructive. With an increasing number of community choirs/groups in many cities desiring to either record or have their independent materials distributed mainstream, there appears to be a major problem with participants receiving a raw deal.

It takes dedication will full commitment, coming together to establish a choir/group, but when there is a source of income, there should be some kind of allocation in consideration of those that are participating. Without the loyalty of those who commit to the choir/group, how are leaders able to accomplish any tasking, especially when leaders of many of these entities can't sing or play an instrument? Anyone can pose as a hype man, verbally shouting out the lyrics of songs as a musical commentator, but it takes talented individuals to perform the musical arrangements demonstrated with style and skill set.

Being overlooked, disregarded, and used will only bring continual frustration to any organization or entity. When leaders embrace this disposition, they will continually experience setbacks and reorganization changes because individuals aren't going for the foolishness anymore. It's painful to work hard and commit yourself to anything, then have someone prostituting your abilities while flaunting luxuries in your face from the essence of your talents/labor. Just imagine if God used us the way we use our brothers and sister and didn't meet our needs. Repentance is applicable right about now!

5.2 Stage Plays and Productions

When a playwright, director, or producer decides to mount a stage play or production, there are many challenging tasks. Understanding the complexity of the genre as it relates to ministry, there are times when playwrights, directors, and producers require help. Locating assistance is generally solicited, requiring freewill, including offers made having earning capacities. It's become common in ministry not to compensate individuals for their time or efforts during the foundation of many endeavors initiated by ministries. Leaders understand that many believe their services to be rewarded by way of sowing (good deeds) their time unto the Lord, which many feel to be good service. Although, many believers contribute time and even money to allow ministries to jump-start

THE PRICE TAG

these kinds of endeavors, there are always those who believe leaders should compensate participants when profits are later accrued.

As producers begin the audition process, locating talented individuals who can fulfill dramatization of a script, leaders tend to target those who don't have professional knowledge of the business. Many seek new talent, who strongly desires an opportunity to demonstrate their abilities with hopes of someone recognizing them and gaining exposure. Having a strong arm of authority over individuals ready to please their leaders; can change the atmosphere having manipulative practices. Innocent hearts, with humbled souls having the desire to please while demonstrating their abilities in hopes of obtaining exposure, many that seek to enter this genre are taken advantage of.

Rehearsals can become time-consuming, and families and other obligations of those participating can become neglected. Although participation within these ministries is freewill, leaders expect and many times demand full support of those who have agreed to participate. Oftentimes, leaders become insensitive about the time they require of others, as there is more to gain/risk for them, rather than those who are fulfilling the work. Cast members and crew become weary not knowing how to explain their frustrations, and many begin to feel guilty when needing to take care of their own personal obligations.

Guilty emotions are often felt as the environment within a stage play or production becomes controlling. Due to the amount of time and money it takes to launch many of these endeavors, leaders become adamant regarding making a profit and enhancing the production. Again, many times the forecasting of these levels doesn't include the compensation of talent, and it later requires more sacrificial time and money from participants. As cast members and crew begin spending additional money for transportation and meals during the production, leaders tend to believe this is part of the freewill option, fulfilling the scope of work. Although, this can progress to several weeks and even months, leaders for some reason tend to disregard financial allocations that participants are investing into their productions. As duties increase, selfish egos tend to rule with a strong arm of authority, and participants are finding themselves reaching further into their pockets in support of many productions.

When are our leaders going to understand that individuals invest into their ministries just as much as they do? When are our leaders going to understand that the stability of any ministry isn't based solely on the man or woman of God who established it? It takes several kinds of functioning individuals having a desire to complete a scope of work to bring success to any entity striving toward a common goal. Therefore, when leaders desire to launch stage plays and production, they should first understand that they couldn't do it alone.

Although hearts of participants remain humble, striving to bring to pass a vision initiated by leaders, it still becomes a hidden burden at times, totally surrendering their will to continue to support. There is a different kind of surrender when we're under the authority of a leader when working freewill, (no compensation) versus being paid to fulfill a scope of work. Participants find themselves battling these kinds of scenarios while struggling with the burden when working freewill. Do our leaders expect the same kind of diligence as if there were compensation attached to our work ethics? Many believe, whether working freewill or by being compensated shouldn't change the efforts used when making a decision to support anything. If someone agrees to fulfill any duty based on presented terms, it then becomes an obligation of the individual to complete it.

When participants find themselves purchasing clothing, accessories, and costumes, further investing into the production, leaders feel it's apart of their freewill responsibility. Although your investment is in support of the ministry, it becomes a part of your agreement to fulfill the scope of work presented. Participants find themselves angry not being aware of all the itemized aspects toward fulfilling their obligation, as it becomes challenging to view the initial vision with the same innocent eyes. Umbrage then makes an impact on the hearts of those, which were once excited about a seemingly great vision, then beginning to corrupt the zeal toward fulfilling further obligation with diligence. Our hearts become hindered when making a decision supporting a ministry, which results to lazy behavior, unfaithfulness, and sporadic diligence including other trends. These feelings tend to become overlooked and never really understood by our leaders, changing the environment for both parties, having the potential to become ugly.

Leaders for some reason still don't understand why participants tend to rebel later after making a commitment to fulfill a duty. Some may tend to judge and/or toss Scripture insinuating the devil being up to something hindering the ministry. Many will ask others to pray for those who begin acting unruly or unfaithful, never once making a phone call or pulling individuals aside to gain understanding. Once an individual begins to feel mistreated or used, feeling they've been tricked or manipulated, it becomes very difficult to reach them. Many individuals within this genre retain frustration. Leaders still haven't been able to reconcile issues, which further progresses into long periods of time having believers on bad terms.

There are touring stage plays and productions that are able to compensate participants for their time rendered to the ministry. In most cases, a promoter implements a weekly pay structure to compensate participants for their talents. In this environment, things tend to change as diligence used toward freewill is often stepped up; now participants are being paid for their abilities.

Leaders at this point can begin implementing business rules and regulations, creating earning capacities contingent upon performance. Many participants transition their freewill attitudes into a now compensative environment, then becoming a business risk to leaders. Leaders become even more adamant when ticket prices, marketing, advertising budgets, and other financial decisions are contingent upon participants. This changes how leaders respond to their participants as things could become aggressive, in which many would be shocked, becoming confused as to what is ministry and what is business. When a scenario of what is ministry verses what is now a business transaction, begins to enters the thinking process of individuals, often times leaders including participants tend to forget the purpose of ministry, as monetary influence becomes priority.

Although, participants are being paid for their abilities used to generate income for production, some leaders retain the same mindset as when individuals were working freewill. What's I'm trying to communicate here is that some leaders tend to withdraw compensation if production doesn't go as planned. Participants have received compromised compensation when leaders experience a loss. With many unexpected and sometimes expected challenges, participants still require full compensation. Working conditions often become unstable, as participants find themselves short of compensation while working on the road. From doubling up in hotel beds to the quality of lodging, this begins to raise a number of complaints from participants who feel politics and fair treatment are present issues.

Leaders are seldom prepared to handle the concerns of angry individuals, especially when there is division amongst a group of people who feels others are being treated differently. Family lines, circle of friends including the conspicuous clicks that hang around, are always just cause of suspicion uncovering segregation. Working within an environment such as this then causes individuals to feel insecure about their positions, appreciation and overall abilities, then initiating speculation regarding our leaders.

Unfortunately, it becomes difficult to get to the root of these kinds of situations, as our leaders are not innocent of the formation and many become involved in them as well. When the environment places a schism in the unity, it becomes the responsibility of our leaders to reconcile and replenish the union. Many times this becomes the preaching opportunity for our leaders to begin indirectly slandering the people regarding being in harmony. Instead of going to individuals directly, leaders tend to get on the microphone, most times swinging abusive analogies, trying to get the people to respond. Why do so many leaders think indirect slander is the way to handle situations? Why are many of our leaders never able to directly reconcile with individuals, but rather become cowards who indirectly try to relay a message?

Talent and crew should gain understanding of this genre before desiring to participate. Many have been known to quit their day jobs, believing touring stage plays, to be a vehicle to stardom. Without solid evidence of an itinerary, many of these ventures are for those who can afford to take a risk on the road. There is no guarantee you will be able to bring home a consecutive weekly salary, as there are times when you're working and times when you're not. The scope of work within many productions is sporadic, so you're better off getting a day job to guarantee income.

Not all productions offer unsecured environments, but knowledge is always key when making decisions that can affect your life tremendously. Having the zeal to share your gift with others is a dynamic heart-driven desire, but there are wolves in the wild ready to prostitute your abilities, sending you home with a bag of souvenirs and internal scars. Although, many feel safe within the sacred forum of what we call ministry, that's where the wolves are building their dens. What a perfect disguise what an undetectable haven, as many leaders have stepped in to use you for gain, instead of the service to and for others.

They will use your initial investment to jump-start the vehicle, requiring dedication and diligence, promising you heaven's best, and then turn you away believing your sin or old sin nature to be a hindrance to the ministry. As mixed emotions trouble the hearts of thousands of believers, many turn away from the Church, including a forum such as this for outreach. Oftentimes, the operations for outreach are different from the structures of local assemblies, but participants are still God's people and should be treated as such. How can abused people reach or service those needing help? How can broken individuals stand confident, having a voice, when our leaders are cracking the whip across their backs?

Many people feel enslaved when working within this forum, being verbally abused and told to give a good performance. Break a leg is not only a theatrical term used in the genre as to wish someone good success, but many have actually tried to break participants legs, probably having an excuse to send them home. Leaders have been known to initiate cruel treatment toward cast members and employees, such as using indirect airline flights and ground transportation that takes someone days to get home. There is no governing source where individuals are able to document complaints, as many outreach ministries are not affiliated with a local assembly. Therefore, participants who agree to presented terms place themselves in full risk of being responsible.

I advise individuals who seek to participate within this genre of outreach to have others look over presented information, which is helpful in making a sound decision affecting your life. Just as leaders will audition and critique your abilities, it's wise to use the same tactics to understand how you're going to be compensated. Committing to hand over a large portion of your time could be rewarding and could be detrimental. It's going to take wisdom to determine if the presented vehicle is the right place to share your talents and abilities, as God will make room for them somewhere else if that's not the place.

With the approach of The Ministry Bureau (read Section 6.2), those who desire to participate in this genre will be able to gain support toward understanding which outreach ministries and/or promoters are signatory and which are not. It's my prayer that you continue to gain understanding regarding the experiences of those in the genre, which can prevent you from making a bad decision. Until you can obtain solid backing, it may be wise to pursue other forums in which your gifts and talents can be used. Without further investigation, talented individuals risk placing their gifts/talents in the hands of pimping wolves, always ready to make another transaction!

5.3 Outreach and Missions
(Domestic and International)

The birth of the Church in the book of Acts (Chapter 2) issues clear instruction for believers to go into the world with the Gospel. Although there are many religions and denominations that embrace this instruction more than others, there remain segregated groups established for missions. Many local assemblies have embraced biblical understanding for outreach, then implementing evangelism auxiliaries. Auxiliaries are typically structured having teams, primarily targeted reaching the surrounding community of the church's neighborhood, including nursing homes and hospitals. Team members pass out religious literature, proclaiming the Gospel of repentance, extending church information, intercessory prayer, including the feeding and clothing of those who require assistance. Evangelism has proven essential because individuals are experiencing life-changing results. Evangelism teams are very significant to local assemblies, as they help increase the potentials for new membership, the rededication of backsliders, as well as ministry functionalities and services offered to its community. It not only reaches within its local area targeting residents, but many times ministries will volunteer members to visit county jails and prisons.

Reaching those who are incarcerated, takes a more strategic approach when desiring to minister to individuals within control of an institutionalized entity. Although this area of evangelism isn't the most popular among those who feel they're called for outreach and missions, there are those who faithfully dedicate their lives reaching those in all areas of life. Week after week, evangelism teams faithfully (having approved dates issued by institutions) visit several county jails, as well as state and federal prisons to share the Gospel with inmates.

Ministries are becoming blind to this area of outreach, as it hasn't occurred there being a tremendous need for pastors and ministers, having fellow believers within these institutions. Although, many are awaiting sentencing or have been convicted of crimes, a need still remains for dedicated individuals to operate a ministry within these walls.

Local pastors may not be aware of many challenges their members experience during outreach endeavors. In general situations, believers are using their own finances toward the

THE PRICE TAG

purchase of food to feed those that may be hungry. When associated with a local assembly, financial allocation should come from the ministry when being apart of its evangelism team. Many ministries have pantries in which members can donate food that can be used for feeding during a ministry's outreach function. It has become common for churches to use these donations when the ministry is conducting its own special events, serving food to its members and visitors. Ministries should stipulate what items can be used for outreach versus what is applicable for its own functionalities. Although churches have special offerings received for outreach and missions, congregants should be aware that monies collected are not typically allocated for these areas. Ministry leaders have been known to use funding in other areas of their ministries. This behavior typically appears manipulative, when congregants begin wondering; *where is the money* when there is a present need. Our leaders are always in position to receive yet another offering when needs arise, as if there is never any money available for the specific needs of ministry.

Transportation costs, supplies, and other necessities required fulfilling many outreach and missions functions are generally not supplied from local assemblies having evangelism groups. This is the primary reason why individuals fail to commit themselves for outreach. Pastors who desire their ministry to extend the function of outreach should begin allocating funding for their evangelism groups. This will meet the needs of team associates, as they are now able to go out and meet the needs of others. Although, there are groups not specifically associated with local assemblies established for outreach and missions, many leaders of these groups typically use their own finances or solicit for donations. These types of ministries are often overlooked, as individual donators are not confident their contributions are going to be used for stated purposes. Therefore, leaders of these groups become focused on seeking other financial sources to support their outreach endeavors.

Unassociated outreach ministries that seek funding to operate their organizations will most likely inquire about obtaining government allocation for their ministry. Although, the ministry may be limited in regards to how they serve within outreach and missions, many will restructure their organizations to comply, meeting requirements to receive government support. With newly proposed business plans, submitted with hopes of receiving grants from the government, leaders have begun targeting the area of transitional/halfway housing. Choosing this category, receiving government funding has proven successful for many ministries whether private and/or a local assembly; but sad to say leaders have seemed to forgotten the core vision for outreach and mission, now becoming expanding business men/women. Within this forum of what many believe is still outreach; individuals who are homeless or have limited income are able to apply for temporary housing.

It's confusing these days to determine what limited income is, or what is considered homeless, many organizations specifically target ex-felons, drug abusers, and homeless singles/couples with children, including battered and abused women. State and federal courts many times will make referrals to these types of organizations, being contingent to pre-sentencing requirements or parole/probation mandatory prerequisites for residents.

Headcounts, date of births, social security numbers, including lengths of stay are the primary profit generator for ministries/organizations maintaining funding. It's common for these organizations to charge residents a portion of their income to qualify for residency. As organizations are still designed to receive donations and other funding support, leaders will continue soliciting their communities, corporation entities, and other sources for donations.

THE PRICE TAG

Sad to say, even with government funding, resident contributions, including corporate and community donations, leaders are still temped by greed. Many organizations have been known to steal corporate donations such as new clothing, bulk snacks and beverages, etc., taking them home to their families rather than distributing them to their residents. Many residents are familiar with this behavior and feel threatened with losing residency, if they interfere with the organizational business affairs. Many will not bite the hand that is feeding them, but many are watching how the food is prepared having the option to eat or not.

With noted corruption within these organizations, it's still common for local assemblies to seek government funding to implement other kinds of outreach functions. Funding extensions are not to be confused with supplying any kind of refuge for congregants, as it's specifically targeted and designed to generate income for the ministry. As congregants are continually solicited to support many extensions, many are not aware it to be funded by government, resident(s) income, including other private donations. This outwardly signifies manipulation, as congregants believe they are supporting specific areas, but is generally, giving in support of what leaders believe to be of equal importance.

There are also non-affiliated organizations and ministries established for missions on domestic and international soil. These entities typically solicit individuals for weekly or monthly contributions to support specific areas for outreach. Having televised programs, even direct mail solicitation campaigns, many of these organizations have been around for decades. Individuals are still confused, as to how these organizations/ministries survive for so long, as they claim to meet the needs of people. Contributors are not aware that these organizations do not completely forward all monies donated to their causes. If you mail or call in a one-time donation (there's no such thing as a one-time donation), weekly or monthly contribution, organizations take a percentage of all monies to operate their businesses. Of course there are organizations which are doing what's right meeting the needs of people, as there are always those that will use this area manipulating people for personal gain.

These kinds of ministries are now expanding, as there appears to be a growing need for financial support on international soil. Congregants worldwide should begin investigating how they're contributing money to these kinds of organizations that claim to support specific areas of missions. There is great speculation (especially in America) about how many organizations are not using their donations toward the areas they claim they support. For example, thereafter September 11, 2001, many organizations jumped up out of nowhere, registering bogus Web sites claiming to support victim relief for this tragedy. Millions of people began contributing to these fraudulent organizations, which has made many of them thousands of dollars without submitting anything toward victim support. Even during the tsunami tragedy in 2005, organizations began doing the same things; corporations even manipulated their own customers. Corporations and organizations began receiving donations from a variety of sources, which didn't make it anywhere but into the books of the company. (I doubt it was even claimed as income.)

Congregants, supporters, and donators must begin investigating where they're sending their money. Just because a sad face on your television screen moves you to be sympathetic to what appears to be a demanding need, it still requires investigation. I can't tell you how many years I've seen thirty-minute programs and thirty to sixty second commercials from organizations soliciting viewers for money. Many have been bold enough to use children with sad, innocent faces, compelling viewers for support. These organizations

THE PRICE TAG

will mail you pictures, letters from children, etc., to acquire financial support. It's sad to even image how many of these organizations are actually ghost entities, making substantial profits utilizing video clips and photos, drawing millions with sympathy; it's very difficult determining who's legit and who's not. We understand that it costs money to operate or maintain anything, but the trick is to avoid educating contributors about how the organization works. Ministries and not-for-profit organizations do not have to list their business financials publicly, but contributors should still investigate.

It's become common for our local assemblies to claim that they're supporting international ventures (sending money overseas), when it's not making its way to specified destinations. If ministries were really supporting many of the ventures they claim they're committed to funding, contributors should be able to check the progress at anytime. Artistic drawings of coming facilities are acceptable in the beginning, soliciting individuals for new construction endeavors, but thereafter, it's necessary that contributors are able to see actual photos and videos of progression to see where their monies are going. If there were no proof, I'd advise all contributors to evaluate why they're supporting a venture.

When contributors begin funding new construction endeavors, I advise them never to give cash. It's very difficult to track or verify the submission of cash. If you desire to contribute to any organization, you may wish to pay with a check to track your support in the event that litigation or manipulation arises. If new construction endeavors are cancelled or not completed, it's your obligation to retrieve your cancelled checks, requesting a refund of your money. No longer tolerate organizations or ministries telling you they're going to use your contributions for other functions of equal importance. This behavior is becoming very common, as leaders are now creating what appear to be bogus plans, proceeding to raise money and then being negligent in completing the work. Some will not even advise you of their business changes, leaving contributors believing the organization/ministry is still making progress.

It's time to begin taking control of our lives, regarding the way we contribute and spend our money! As contributors and consumers, we must be aware that entities feel there is a tremendous need to manipulate us, taking our opinions and decisions away. This behavior truly leaves individuals victimized, controlled, not in control of their lives. We all have our own decisions to make, and when others, who are not initiating sound choices in our best interests, are making them for us, you can truly expect individuals to be maltreated. We understand the Bible teachings of it being better to give than to receive, but giving doesn't mean being blind, tricked, or uneducated about where your money is being allocated.

Many organizations will tell you exactly what you want to hear. As it's becoming common for leaders asking us for all of our personal business, proceeding to market according to our needs (what we're lacking). Don't be quick to tell your personal information to organizations that are trying to win sales. Consumers are giving too much information before hearing or being educated about a product or service. If you begin telling a sales executive all your problems, he or she will try selling you everything according to your requirements. Investigate products and services before purchasing anything. Never purchase from any organization without being educated first. Call two to three times and ask many questions before making a transaction. When individuals hang the phone up on you or refuse to talk to you, it's obvious they were not concerned about educating you about

THE PRICE TAG

their products or services, but only wanted to get your credit card number or check. (It's sad to say, many sales executives are not even educated themselves about the products/services they offer.)

When dealing with religious organizations and ministries, many leaders are not concerned about aftercare, only regarding making another transaction or maintaining funding. Our leaders are always searching to reach further into outreach, with hopes of finding new ways to take out a profit! It's your obligation to begin reaching into your heart, always discovering what's wise and relevant to how you're giving and supporting religious ventures. There's nothing wrong with not giving when being asked, for there is always time to support later. If there is no peace as it relates to giving, you're not giving in the right direction or from a joyous heart.

CHAPTER SIX

AUTHOR'S DELIBERATION
6.1 Calling All Members of the Body of Christ

Congregants are growing weary with several issues that affect our assemblies; many have chosen to intercede in prayer, while others have continued to complain. It's imperative that we get back to praying for our pastors and/or ministry leaders. Without prayer, we cannot expect them to uphold a balanced ministry. Our duty as believers is to be a praying people. Without prayer, our spiritual empowerment decreases, supplying believers with limited resource when in need.

Increasingly, many of our leaders have converted the House to function as a dictatorship. Many of our present assemblies have become exclusively about what the pastor desires for the House. Many congregants have confused their accolades to God versus what he or she gives to the man or woman of God over the House. This behavior seems contagious, as now our ministry leaders have begun using this as a pedestal for control. Congregants have become quick calling the titles of the man or woman of God, verses responding to the simple command of "Praise the Lord."

THE PRICE TAG

Our identity as believers has diminished, including our identifying language. We're no longer able to speak have a peculiar identity; we've compromised our positions, adapting our language to trendy concepts and ways, believing this to help reach non-believers.

We must begin praying that our leaders get back to their positions in the Body of Christ, no longer standing before God's people as a substitute for the Holy Ghost! This statement appears stern, but this is the position of many of our assemblies, as congregants increasingly desire to speak of more title, status, and positions disregarding the Holy Spirit, which is the functioning source of the Body of Christ at large!

It's time we get back to praying that our ministry leaders give glory to God. It's okay to pray for the success of your ministry, but also be led by the Spirit to pray that our leaders give all glory and honor to God. Many leaders forget about the things of the Kingdom and begin taking the credit and glory for themselves. Don't forget what Paul taught us: *But God forbid that I should glory, save in the cross of our Lord Jesus Christ, by whom the world is crucified unto me, and I unto the world.* (Galatians 6:14)

Many of our leaders don't know how to handle opposition. Our society unfortunately has conditioned us to be quick to offense, criticism, even physical harm to those that undermine our lives and even ministries. When focusing on our calling and purpose, we must always understand that we're not exempt from criticism and personal attack. *Blessed are ye, when men shall revile you, and persecute you, and shall say all manner of evil against you falsely, for my sake. Rejoice, and be exceeding glad: for great is your reward in heaven: for so persecuted they the prophets which were before you.* (Matthew 5:11-12)

It has always been our commission to pray that our leaders retain compassionate hearts. There should be absolutely no reason for hundreds of thousands of congregants to stay home rather than worshipping in their assemblies. The hearts of our leaders are growing insensitive to the needs and desires of hurting people. Jesus has given us clear instruction regarding ministry, as our leaders should be position for service, but now they're in position for big business. Many don't even think twice about verbally abusing God's people or telling them to leave their church. Many of our leaders deal with God's people as if we have leprosy or other contagious diseases. But Christ Jesus was clear as He sent out His followers with instruction: *Heal the sick, cleanse the lepers, raise the dead, cast out devils: freely ye have received freely give.* (Matthew 10:8)

Is your ministry leader concerned about lost congregants? If so, why hasn't he commissioned people to go after them? I'm not talking about those congregants that aren't concerned about church, but those that have found fault with a ministry. There doesn't seem to be a concern about those individuals, as it's a challenge to pursue reconciliation when someone may have a valid reason for leaving a ministry. We should begin praying that our leaders strive to be concerned about the lost. Again: not only those that don't know God, but those who are wandering without a pastor, due to present and/or former situations affecting many ministries.

In addition, many of our leaders are still not concerned for those that still remain unbelievers. As the proclamation of the Good News of Jesus Christ, have become the occasional message and prosperity and success, has become the weekly banner for millions of congregants. As Christians, we cannot deny people outside of Christ; for we all have been given the ministry of reconciliation. It's our duty as believers, not leaving this responsibility solely up to our leaders, but sharing our testimonies and triumphs with others that will draw them to the same cross in which we believe. (II Corinthians 5:18)

Don't ever cease to pray that our assemblies remain focused on Christ. Our society will continue to grow compulsive, therefore prompting our ministries to infiltrate common psychology, including doctrine that feels good but has no conviction to believers. Our sanctuaries are overflowing these days with congregants who have forgotten why they even attend church. It's becoming common that leaders are conditioning the House, supplying comfort for those that seek this compromised atmosphere. If the House doesn't point people to the cross, how can it call or establish itself as a ministry?

Our prayers in regards to temptation shouldn't be far from our lips, as our leaders are increasingly finding themselves with present issues. Lust of the flesh, lust of the eyes, and the pride of life are the primary causes affecting our leaders and even us as believers. Our flesh desires more and more, but if you feed your eyes the things that will nurture the flesh, including placing your ears on similar things that will increase temptations of the flesh, you will continually become out of control. God help us all when our leaders are out of control, turning a death ear to correction or awareness.

It's imperative that our leaders understand that quiet time for personal devotion is a priority. Many don't manage a balanced life or understand the need for centering into the Spirit. With all the services, conventions, and other functions that our leaders supposedly established for fundraising and other motives, it has become extremely difficult for them to take a break to refresh their direction or vision. Having a loss of personal devotion will ambush the ministry, including the family of our leaders. It shouldn't take sickness in your body or a breakdown of health to tell you that something is lacking. Don't disregard personal devotion for personal gain. You won't be able to retain your possession, as it will slip away like sand in a windstorm. Having no focus, clear direction, balance, physical strength, or peace, reveals a negative outcome for our leaders; which they require so much to lead us as God's people. Therefore, we must pray earnestly that our leaders maintain their necessities. Now, does this mean sending them on a cruise every three months? No! If your leaders desire to go on a cruise every three months, then let them pay for it out of their own pockets.

It sometimes becomes difficult for our leaders to know the will of God for every situation. Therefore, it's our duty to pray that God's will is revealed. Obtaining revelation as it relates to specific instruction from God will only place a peaceful environment in the House. When we feel confused, speculating what the man or woman of God is telling us, and this should let us know that possibly our leaders aren't clear about God's leading. Just as we become unclear about God's will at times, our leaders face similar situations. That's why we should always pray that our leaders understand God's will, for if not, they'll lead us in the wrong direction. *For this cause we also, since the day we heard it, do not cease to pray for you, and to desire that ye might be filled with the knowledge of His will in all wisdom and spiritual understanding.* (Colossians 1:9)

Your leader may preach the roof off the building but he or she still needs to be empowered by the Holy Spirit on a continual basis. He or she may be a great teacher, organizer, businessman or businesswoman, and counselor, but without the power of the Holy Spirit, there is no significant value to be accomplished through the ministry. Money, gifts, anniversaries, appreciations services, new cars, homes, jewelry, and trips around the world cannot empower our leaders to be effective in ministry. It's going to take the power of the Holy Ghost, just as it does with our lives. Without it, your leader may seek an alternative outcome for demonstration. We've seen enough tricks and hocus-pocus in our sanctuaries; we need to experience increased levels of the Holy Ghost.

Our leaders need to be protected as well. Taking a stand for Christ becomes a target of the enemy; therefore, we have to say a prayer of protection. Paul has asked God's people to pray for him, but our leaders shouldn't have to ask us to pray, for this should be an automatic commission as a believer. *Obey them that have the rule over you, and submit yourselves: for they watch for your souls, as they that must give account, that they may do it with joy, and not with grief: for that is unprofitable for you.* (Hebrews 13:17) *And for me, that utterance may be given unto me, that I may open my mouth boldly, to make known the mystery of the Gospel. For which I am an ambassador in bonds: that therein I may speak boldly, as I ought to speak.* (Ephesians 6:19-20)

Many times we become annoyed with our leaders and don't even pray for them. We simply forget or aren't interested, but this is our duty as believers. As the purpose of this book is to bring change to the Body of Christ at large, we must change as well! When we position ourselves to be responsible to our duty and commission, we can expect situations with our leaders to change too. Don't sit back expecting things to change instantly; maybe it's time for you to change first. Maybe you're in the wrong ministry, or possibly you're not in concordance with the vision of ministry. There could be several areas we as believers need to evaluate to better understand our position in Christ Jesus. Without position, you're not ready or fit for purpose.

I'm calling all members of the Body of Christ to get back to prayer within the House of Prayer. Begin praying for the lost, praying for our leaders, and praying for the message of this book to penetrate the hearts of believers around the world. As you begin praying, I'm sure God will show you all the areas in your assembly that need investigation and possible restructuring. Not everyone can do the same thing, and not everyone has an identical purpose. I'm challenging you to discover your purpose.

By the next volume of this book, I should have been able to document progress and see how believers around the world have committed themselves to get the House of Prayer back in order. Most likely, it's going to start with our leaders, but if not, congregants should be equipped to make sound decisions regarding the ministries they're attached to. It's time to start cleaning up our assemblies. If the House isn't right, then you shouldn't be there, or your duty is to stay, working with others to clean it up.

Many leaders are not going to like this progressive effort to clean up the House. Many are happy with the confusion, animosities, and other situations that handicap our ministries from doing a great work for the Kingdom. When you run into leaders that are kicking against the pricks, (rebelling) it's not your duty to fight or disrespect them but to pray. If that become a real situation, I'm pretty sure you'll be able to connect with other believers, as there is so much work that requires your talent and your abilities that are useful to the Body of Christ. Your help is needed, and it's not going to be measured by money or demographic; it's going to be rewarded by your willing heart saying, "Yes, Lord, I'll do my part." That was what I said when writing this book. Now it's your turn! **WHAT CAN YOU PERSONALLY DO TO HELP BRING AWARENESS TO THE CHANGES AFFECTING THE BODY OF CHRIST?**

6.2 Get Your House in Order
(Serving Those Who Serve)

THE MINISTRY BUREAU

The Ministry Bureau establishment will represents choir members, praise and worship singers, ushers, musicians, clergy, deacons, sanctuary helpers, and drama affiliates within the areas of sanctuary worship, outreach and missions, Christian and gospel music, as well as other areas of ministry. The Bureau will operate similar to a union, helping its members receive adequate payment for their services rendered in the areas of ministry. The Bureau plans to establish compliance, creating policies guaranteeing its members weekly compensation (if working weekly) for all services rendered to a local assembly, outreach or missions ministry. Guaranteed compensation can only be earned while working for entities who are signatory with The Bureau. Non-signatory entities may employ a Bureau member, but the Bureau wouldn't secure any kind of compensation, as the entity wouldn't be approved.

Approved signatory entities will be required to pay all Bureau members pension and health credits (fee), including Bureau fees along with member compensation for services rendered to the entity. The Bureau will create guidelines assisting its members when making ministry decisions when search signatory vs. non-signatory entities. The Bureau will require all churches who are signatory to issue all Bureau members pay for their participation for work rendered in sanctuary worship from: singing on a choir, praise and worship singers, ushers, musicians, drama affiliates, technicians, clergy, trustee including deacons. The Bureau will require all record labels that have Christian/gospel music divisions to issue each participating Bureau member payment for work rendered on a music project. Each project must be pre-negotiated, having a listed fee for payment to Bureau members. The Bureau will require all outreach and missions entities that are signatory to issue pay to Bureau members for work rendered in missions from evangelism to prisons, hospitals, and street teams, as well as outreach choirs and singing groups (consisting of members from different churches) and drama affiliates (stage plays, dance groups, and theatrical events).

The Bureau will set a minimum hourly pay rate to be applied across all areas of ministry (for members that serve in multiple areas). Signatory entities will not be allowed to pay below the established minimum hourly rate, but can pay above the noted minimum rate to any member if desired. The Bureau will require all signatory entities to pay a percentage of the total accrued weekly salary as a union fee, including a percentage for members' pension and health funds.

Those having a desire to become members of the Ministry Bureau will be required to join by established, approved membership. Applicants seeking to receive compensation for work rendered in the area of ministry are required to be members of a local assembly for more than twelve months. Your membership must be verified before being approved for membership in the Bureau. If there are unfaithful or otherwise noted stipulations or no established congregational history, applicants must wait to be verified before being approved to join the Ministry Bureau. Applicants must have completed their local assembly's new-member orientation and all required classes offered to new congregants before qualification for approved status. Upon approved status, the applicant will be required to pay an annual membership fee, which will give members access to numerous resources and benefits.

The Ministry Bureau will not guarantee that your local assembly and/or other signatory entities will employ members, but will secure adequate working conditions, including fair pay, for services rendered in ministry. Signatory entities will then be able to structure areas of their ministry having sanctioning for members that show up late, uncooperative, present risk to ministry operation or business. Entities will be able to deduct from members weekly pay for occurrences that are against Bureau policies and procedures. This will help thousands of ministries initiate order within their assemblies. Although, members may seek to join several auxiliaries, trying to make a living on ministry, signatory entities will be able to implement member restrictions.

The Ministry Bureau will render weekly pay, collecting total hours worked for all members, including fees and credits from each signatory entity. Although members will be obligated to their local assembly, the Bureau will become a secondary point of contact if there is ever a situation within the assembly affecting its members. Members will be able to submit confidential claims regarding corrupt or abrupt changes affecting their local assembly, as the assembly must be a signatory entity. Members that choose to change assemblies should resituate themselves with other signatory assemblies, therefore making sure Bureau services and policy will be valid. The Bureau will serve in the best interest of its members and signatory entities, creating a presence in local areas to implement the large areas of serve needed for success.

Volume II of The Price Tag will introduce additional information, which will begin to penetrate the areas of ministry that earnestly need help. Although this plan seems far from us, it's going to take this kind of overseeing organization to make sure it serves and protects those who serve in ministry. If those who serve in ministry are being mistreated, abused, and turned away, what can we expect to see in the coming years? As diligent as I am to get this volume and two others to you, I ask that you reflect the same diligence toward the implementation of The Ministry Bureau.

(Sample)

SIGNATORY INTERVIEW SCRIPT

(ALL PHONE CONVERSATIONS WILL BE RECORDED)

Opening: It's a glorious day in the Bureau my name is_____. How can I help you today?

1. Am I speaking with the pastor of the church to become signatory?
2. Are you an associate pastor, having a senior pastor you report to?
3. May I have the name of the senior pastor that is responsible for you?
4. May I have your full legal name?
5. May I ask your date of birth please?
6. Do you go by any other names?
7. What is your current ordained title?
8. May I have the name of the individual who ordained you?
9. Do you remember the date in which you were ordained?
10. In what city, state, and county were you ordained?
11. Do you remember the name of the church where you were ordained?
12. Were you elected pastor of your church, or are you the founder?
13. If elected, can I have the name(s) of the responsible person(s), who makes election decisions?
14. How long have you been pastor of your assembly?
15. What is the full name of the church, which you pastor?
16. May I ask what denomination (if any) your assembly would be associated?
17. Are you satisfied with the denominational affiliation or do you wish to become nondenominational?
18. Do you know how long the church has been in establishment?
19. What is the church's street address? Is there a suite or building number?

20. What city, state, and postal/zip Code?
21. Is there a different mailing address for the ministry?
22. What are the main telephone/fax numbers for the church?
23. May I have your direct line to your church office (if any)?
24. What is the name of your assistant/secretary?
25. Do you currently have other employees in the ministry?
26. Are they paid weekly or biweekly (or other)?
27. Are employees paid by payroll or with cash?
28. Do you offer employees any fringe benefits?
29. What kinds of fringe benefits are offered?
30. Do you utilize the services of a payroll company, or are paychecks generated within the ministry?
31. Are you confident today that you're making a wise decision becoming signatory with The Ministry Bureau?
32. Can you tell me how you believe the Bureau will assist your ministry?

Bureau Code of Ethics

6.3 Our Leaders

Without question, there is a tremendous need for change. Not being able to pinpoint every occurrence and/or situation, which affects the Body of Christ, I've still outlined a great scope of work that requires ministry leaders to comply. Would leaders believe there is a present issue within their assembly? Some will be able to identify their issues, and others will remain in denial. As this publication is released as a tool for congregants to evaluate their positions and approach to ministries, which they support, you will most likely begin to see immediate changes impacting ministries on a weekly basis.

Many ministry leaders will have to stand before their assemblies begging for forgiveness, others will have to resign from their leadership positions, and some ministries will fold up. These coming changes will be out of my control, as I'm only a messenger, being obedient to what was sown and nurtured in my heart. Leaders in full-time ministry may have to brush up on their skills, returning to full-time employment due to a decrease in financial support. Evangelist, whom makes a living traveling for the sake of the Gospel, may have to find alternative ways increasing your earning capacities, as I believe your phone may not ring as often. Those, whom are situated toward congregational growth including, having building fund endeavors in place, may need to pull back from some of your financial targets, as congregants will begin pulling back their finances.

Am I encouraging congregants to stop supporting ministry, which will cause business entities to experience hardship? No! I've clearly through this publication have supplied congregants and/or other supporters with awareness that has been needed for so long. For years, millions of people, have tried to find ways of slandering the Church or by striking controversy regarding those whom represent The Kingdom of God, but none has ever been able to strike controversy, deliver awareness while offering solution(s) even funding them; oh yes, I will be funding The Ministry Bureau.

If I've offended anyone or caused any unforeseen situations for any ministry, I openly apologize. I will not be able to continually offer my apologies, as changes will begin affecting ministries. I sympathize with much of the hard work and dedication that has been applied over many years, building ministries to the levels in which they appear, but restructuring must take place. I cannot forecast any other way to communicate to you that this message is going to put many of you on your knees, as some will experience great loss. Too many believers have been calling on God, crying in the shadows of praise, not knowing how to break loose from the bondages that some of your ministries have placed on the people. You must know God isn't going to sit back allowing His beloved/chosen people to remain victims of those who represent him.

If more leaders would have had the tenacity to take a stand, possibly things could have been moving in a different direction. Many only become concerned and motivated when situations have affected their personal incomes or households, but when it's someone else's burden, they observe from a distance and say, "I'll be praying for you," while not praying at all.

There isn't much any of us can do in regards to the walls of denomination, but it's going to take leaders within these walls to begin the restructuring process for all assemblies under denominative umbrellas. The coming establishment of The Ministry Bureau will not collaborate with any particular individual; therefore, leaders may desire to gain notoriety through the entity. The Bureau will be a corporate entity that will structure ministry compliance throughout all areas of ministry. I will effectively organize validated individuals to secure Human Resource endeavors that will prevent the Bureau from become tainted by denomination, ethnicity and/or other segregated wall. Leaders and congregants will equally be able to utilize the Bureau for all services in which it's designed, meeting the needs of individuals.

I'm encouraging leaders not to fight against the Bureau when it begins to penetrate communities, as those that serve in ministry are going to be aware of its foundation. Many leaders will choose not to become signatory as there will be no pressure, but those who serve in your ministry will begin to wonder why you have no desire to offer them something, as they've been an asset to your ministry. This decision can cause your supporters to make alternative decisions regarding how they're supporting your ministry.

I'm encouraging ministry leaders to use this message as a way of reconciliation. It's easy to take offense, but it's very difficult to make a decision for reconciliation. Your community is in need of reconciliation, as many feel that pastors and leaders only look out for themselves. Whatever happened to the days when evangelism teams went door-to-door? Although, the Jehovah's Witness religion specializes in this area of outreach, their tactics are known to be aggressive and annoying. They're now spending so much of their time trying to convince people (mostly Christians) that their doctrine is false. Why are they spending so much time standing around hold their publications in their nice plastic holders (most times judging individuals) trying to convince believers that their religion/doctrine is the only way to God? I believe they should revisit their foundation as well, as there are millions of complaints about them too.

People are faced with too many situations on a weekly to monthly basis regarding religion. There are new doctrines and denominations and all kinds of practices coming to the forefront, yet no one seems concerned about how these ministries are impacting God's people. It's hard to reach an individual who has been scorched by a ministry, and many leaders turn their faces from these things to avoid having to take a stand. We know that you will lose popularity and many times financial support, but you're going to lose it anyway for not taking a stand. Congregants are going to be making wise decisions because leaders have been cowards over God's people.

It troubles me how many leaders choose to mentor others who will one day lead God's people in many directions. What will be the outcome of these paths, as many will go forth as carbon copies, implementing destruction and compromise into the House? Many of us can see it now with the young people who are stepping up, believing they're doing a great work for the Kingdom. Several of our soon coming leaders have no clue about purpose, having no vision or real message; just flipping through Scriptures with hopes of finding something catchy, stirring the people for a good offering. Guess where they've learned this—from those who trained and mentored them into the same foolishness in which they're operating.

What's going to be so surprising about this book is that it's going to be a tool for early preachers and teachers, and even those who have been teaching and preaching for years. You'll be surprise how this publication is going to revolutionize more preachers than expected. I dare you to use this publication for reconciliation and education, bringing awareness for all congregants. I believe this publication should be a mandatory tool for new beginners, even new congregants joining a ministry. When empowering new congregants and believers with such a message, I guarantee you'll begin creating a balanced ministry. My belief is that individuals will receive an educational tool from the gate, then being able to utilize the information or turning from it being careless. But I believe individuals should make the decision how to use it.

New believers and congregants are the most sought after victims, as they don't know the game as well as seasoned believers. It can take nearly three to five years before they begin to notice practices that ambush our assemblies, and most times they're out the door before anyone misses them. Unfortunately, many ministries don't even care about the turnover within their assemblies, but they'll still count the number of individuals as current members, although they're no longer attending. Why do leaders mention having several thousands members as many only have half, in which regularly attend?

It's time leaders begin reorganization and restructuring. There are serious issues that exist, and congregants and others are now becoming aware of exactly how ministries operate. It's time for you to pull together, because many of you will have to consolidate your ministries, as each will experience change. To alleviate several dissolved ministries, it may be best to consolidate and create a balanced ministry versus having a struggling entity, which will most likely have to pressure its existing congregants to survive. It's time to roll up your sleeves and evaluate the need for compliance. It doesn't only exist by way of our biblical examples, in which many still choose to compromise. I can only begin to speculate of coming changes, giving suggestive thinking to prevent severe hardship, but no one really knows until the time will come, when situations begin to impact your ministry. Don't begin threatening your congregants about their obligations, with a motive of finding fault with this publication, as this is the tool that millions have been waiting for to become a voice for the voiceless.

Your congregants will instantaneously see you in real colors as you stand before them speaking contrary to the message of this publication. I urge you again to use this as a tool for reconciliation, as love will cover the multitude of sin. As many are guilty and could possibly deserve what many of us are too Christian to image, I encourage you to reach toward love, being reminded of your position as stewards over God's people. This can supply a way of escape for many of you who, through only God's mercy, will survive.

As we begin to further examine layers of unheard situations, as thousands of congregants are going to come forth out of nowhere, you will clearly see how this message has been swept under the rugs for decades. I already know that my heart will not be able to stand all the stories of congregants trying to communicate their personal situations, inflicted by ministry, which have ambushed their lives. Therefore, I will become silent during that period as many will look for me to supply comforting as the person, which delivered the initial message. Leaders, it's your responsibility to reconcile with your members. If one of your members comes forth, it's time to get in the mud to clean off the sheep. You have to reach back into your communities and revisit your evangelism strategies. I know you've thought that dressing down, wearing sneakers and T-shirts and baseball caps, was going to reach the lost, but has it worked?

I dare you to put those choir robes back on and revamp all of the sanctuary celebratory aspect for ministry (this includes Holy Communion and Baptism). Watch how your ministry will shift, which is going to be the first step toward preparing for a reconciliation/revival movement. You're going to have to position your assembly to be prepared for the lost to return. You're going to have to educate ushers how to handle congregants which are disrespecting the House with their dress codes and more. Get back to the code of ethics regarding dress codes in the sanctuary. I'm not talking about bondages that used to plague sanctuaries in the former days; I'm talking about proper attire.

THE PRICE TAG

Without order, you won't be able to expect any progress in your ministry. Our assemblies, including its leaders, have been out of control for so long. By now this has compelled you to understand that you are included into all the changes that will begin to surface year after year. Your duties are not exempt, and your position as a leader shouldn't be withdrawn. If you can lead individuals from behind a pulpit, you should have no problem adjusting to change, if you're not in position to preach on a weekly basis. I challenge leaders to begin monthly discussion forums, including their congregants, so the ministry can pull together and strengthen the body. This will ensure that all are in compliance with the vision, gaining understanding toward improvement and restructure.

It's my prayer that these aspects for change are viewed with eyes of wisdom, being able to launch a powerful attack on the enemy. If he can destroy the Church from the inside out (have mercy), imagine what is to come with a negative destructive impact. This is a serious message that leaders should begin to reconcile, strengthen their organizational structures, launch their evangelism forces, celebrate the return of the lost, and go higher into the next levels of where the ministry is headed. Without a plan, I don't see much success for your ministry in the coming years.

Congratulations to all those who have an ear to hear what the Spirit is saying to the Church. I celebrate all of my brothers and sisters who are able to embrace this message and are striving to make a difference in the place, the center, creating an eternal difference for a believer. The scope of work isn't just to clean up immediate situations, but is established having the capacity to eventually out live us all as long as the return of our Lord remains in coming time. There isn't much we can do about those who are no longer with us, that desired to language their concerns, but we can prepare a better way for those that are present and will come after us, needing this new foundation, creating better ministries and believers around the world.

The world's way of thinking couldn't give this to you having compassion, correction and solution on one plate, for you must know this is the heart of the one that has called us all to Himself. Embrace His way, capture His voice, and press toward His mark, knowing there is great reward that cannot compare to all your product offers and/or ministry services you can ever offer. Just as many go to the gym to work on several areas of their body, it's time we begin working on the Body of Christ—each one doing its part, each part functioning as it should to get the work done.

When these changes start to usher progress throughout the lands of the world, watch how there will be revival all over the place. Wait until you hear the new songs that will burst forth from this message. You haven't celebrated until you've seen or heard the testimonies that will come from leaders, yet alone congregants. Begin to invest in your congregants; they're your only real assets. Honor them for all the diligent support they have given over many years to the ministry. Don't forget we have a choice, and our choices are always relevant, as there are other alternatives.

To all my brothers and sisters that carry the Gospel or particular messages from God, don't give up on your message. Don't believe your message isn't relevant or needed. We don't develop messages as such; the Holy Spirit nurtures these kinds of messages in our hearts for years, until it's time to come forth, making the impact as designed. Carry your message, and allow the Holy Spirit to nurture it year after year, for the time will come that it must come forth for harvest. Always remember that your blessing is contingent on your obedience. For many years, I've been seeking several things, but it wasn't until I was able to be obedient to what God was nurturing in my life, then being able to receive all the things which were contingent upon my obedience. I challenge you to do the same. Be obedient to your call, and He will give you all the things your heart seeks.

If congregants are now paying for the Word, it's because leaders have taken the wrong position representing God. As each congregant will continue to be faced with this question, it's up to you to educate your followers so they should have an answer to this question and every other that requires an answer. Until next time, I salute you with the Kingdom's best wishes and resources, having already received the possession that equips us with everything we need to fulfill purpose. Let the Church/Ecclesia say Amen and Amen!

AUTHOR'S BIO

The Believer's Biography States:

"For we all have come from, to...
And we're all going into, for..."

I'm only a congregant, just like you!

REPRESENTATION

NEW INTERNATIONAL MANAGEMENT AGENCY

Phone: +1 (678) 441-0700
Fax: +1 (678) 441-0760
Website: www.NIMA-AGENCY.com

AUTHOR'S CONTACT INFORMATION

D'Morea E. Johnson
P.O. Box 495
New York, NY 10163-0495

Email: mail4dmorea@aol.com
Website: www.DMOREAJOHNSON.com